Laughter Ten Years After

Jo Anna Isaak, Curator

Essays by
Jo Anna Isaak
Jeanne Silverthorne
Marcia Tucker

Hobart and William Smith Colleges Press 1995

Editor: Jo Anna Isaak
Laughter Ten Years After, catalogue, 1995.

Hobart and William Smith Colleges Press
Geneva, New York 14456

Design: Dan Miller Design, New York
Copy editor: Avis Lang
Printed in an edition of 1,500 by Becotte and Gershwin, Inc.

ISBN 0-910969-027

Contents

Introduction

Let me say straight away — this is a retro show, a re-play. Why this urge to repeat? An obsession to revise and rewrite, to get it right? Yes, in part, and along with that the realization that the impulse is utopian in the sense of being both hopeful and infinite — the work being produced is far in excess of what can be included in any one exhibition. A commemoration: something important has happened in the past decade, and this is an occasion for celebration. A chance to take stock: the way we look at the past often determines the way we go into the future. A feeling of solidarity: the ideological self-realization that a number of women — without being part of a group, working in different media and in different countries, addressing disparate concerns — are nevertheless able to speak surprisingly clearly of our collective agenda. Even if we have never met, we have become confident of the shared aims of our collective, and we have come to realize how one woman's work or words leads onto or enables the next woman to work or speak. A sense of loss: the realization that women's history is faintly written and must be continually re-inscribed before it is forgotten again. And then of course, as Gertude Stein knew, one always needs to repeat because, "Every time it is so, it is so, it is so."

In 1982 I organized an exhibition entitled "The Revolutionary Power of Women's Laughter" in an attempt to locate art within the arena of contemporary theoretical discussions. The fundamental discoveries of modern linguistics and psychoanalysis had radically affected the understanding of how all signifying systems operate. There was growing awareness that a great deal was at stake for women in these new assessments of how meaning is produced and organized in all areas of cultural practice. The death of the author leveled the playing field for women — and play in the new, authority-free zone they did. Over the past decade there has erupted a riot of women artists exploring the potential of laughter, hysteria, the grotesque and the carnivalesque.

To gather a group of women artists together under any rubric is to be forced into an essentialist position. Group shows of exclusively male artists, by contrast, are allowed to address whatever organizing principle the curator has in mind: a geographical location the artists may have in common, a period of time in which they worked, a particular style or medium. Women artists, writers, and curators have never been able to masquerade in the Emperor's clothes of universal humanity. Even if only two women artists are exhibited together, the issue of gender inevitably arises. But to engage in a strategic, rather than a predetermined, essentialism is to push the issue of gender past the point where it can be used to ghettoize women.

I am not attempting in this exhibition to present The Most Important contemporary women artists. The artists in the exhibition may or may not be part of what has been mythologized as the mainstream. I am not interested in valorizing a mainstream nor in exploring, validating, and reinforcing hegemony, which, as Raymond Williams points out, is a process that relies upon the mechanisms of tradition and the canons of Old Masters in order to waylay the utopian desires that are potentially embodied in cultural production. *The waylaid utopian desires are what I'm interested in.*

These artists are women who did not cede their desire. They began by dismantling "the prison house of language" through play, or laughter, or, to use the term the French have reintroduced into English, jouissance: enjoyment, pleasure, particularly sexual pleasure or pleasure derived from the body. They explored Bakhtin's theory of laughter and the carnivalesque as potential sites for social insurgency; Barthes's and Kristeva's notion of laughter as libidinal license, the jouissance of the polymorphic, orgasmic body; Freud's analysis of the liberation of laughter in the workings of a witticism or a play upon language. They reveled in their primary narcissism — the one characteristic some women have that men lack. They exposed the viewer to the terror of their irreparable difference. They donned the masks of the masquerade, or they went too far and took them all off. They enlisted the hysterics gesture of resistance, or they became grotesques. They put on gorilla masks and marched on the museums. If, in the process, they have established reputations in the mainstream, they have done so by undermining the very characteristics upon which it is established. Their success is important for the way it has changed contemporary thinking about value systems that extend far beyond the art world. Using the subversive strategy of humor, they have radically reformulated contemporary art and called into question art history's long-held verities concerning creativity, genius, mastery, and originality. Their critique of art history and theoretical reflections on gender, sexuality, politics, and representation have shattered central assumptions about art and its relation to society.

Laughter, as it is invoked in this exhibition, is meant to be thought of as a metaphor for transformation, a catalyst for cultural change. In providing libidinal gratification, laughter can also provide an analytic for understanding the relationships between the social and the symbolic while allowing us to imagine these relationships differently. In asking for the response of laughter, these artists are engaging in a difficult operation. The viewer must want, at least briefly, to emancipate himself from "normal" representation; in order to laugh, he must recognize that he shares the same repressions. What is requested is not a private, depoliticized jouissance but sensuous solidarity. Laughter is first and foremost a communal response and at the same time an acknowledgement of liberation.

Throughout the time I have been working on this project I have felt I was working on a collective. I am grateful to all the artists who contributed their work to the exhibition and to Jeanne Silverthorne and Marcia Tucker for their essays. I want to express my deep sense of gratitude to Marcia for her years of work and commitment to projects like these. Many people worked on this exhibition. I am particularly grateful to Avis Lang, Susan Unterberg, Klaus Ottmann, and Hank McNeil for their help and for the reassurance of their commitment to this project; like laughter, confidence is among the highly infectious expressions of psychical states.

The American essayist Barbara Ehrenreich once wrote that the United States in the 1950s was characterized by the attitude that "God gave women uteruses and men wallets." Women faced considerable discrimination due to the postwar retrenchment of patriarchal values, and by the late 1960s there was growing awareness of the nature of that discrimination.

As a curator at the Whitney Museum of American Art at that time and also a member of the early radical feminist group RedStockings, I became concerned with the small number of

marginalized because of their age.

Those of us who were activist art critics or curators faced problems that made it difficult to put our views into practice. We encountered sexist attitudes, ranging from the blatant to the seemingly unconscious, on the part of directors, editors, and colleagues. And in the press, on panels, and at demonstrations, the community of artists — rightly feeling powerless — often attacked those working from within institutions to promote change, the assumption being that we could not be feminists.

From Muse to Museum: Late 20th Century Feminism
and Artistic Practice in the United States

women represented in the Whitney's exhibitions. Consequently, my women colleagues and I began to do what we could to visit women's studios, include more women in exhibitions, write critically about their work, and situate ourselves within the larger community of women.

Feminists at that time saw clearly that "the personal is the political," but we were all practice and no theory. We drew the battle lines as women against men, but we didn't stop to ask — or didn't yet have the distance and experience to ask — what kind of system had created the inequities between us in the first place. Nor did we ask why the women's movement was largely white, heterosexual, and upper middle-class or how issues of race and sexual orientation intersected with those of gender.

Nonetheless, there was progress. Throughout the 1970s many women artists who are now well known in the United States began to exhibit. Even so, although most were doing unorthodox and intellectually challenging work, they were generally overshadowed by men whose work was far less adventurous. The younger artists who are most visible today were graduate students then and had to contend with a discriminatory university and art school system. Older artists were

SO WE WERE DIVIDED:

between women seen as wielding power from within the system and women who felt victimized by that power and that system;

between those who advocated aesthetic separatism — who saw round, open, fluid forms, soft colors, obsessive patterning, and craft skills as inherently feminine (and their opposite as inherently masculine) — and those who insisted that art has no gender;

between "special interest" groups — such as lesbian artists who felt isolated from heterosexual women by virtue of both their politics and distinct concerns reflected in their work — and the dominant feminist culture;

between white, middle-class women in the arts and women of color, for whom the situation was even more critical, since there was almost no forum for either the work or the ideas of Black, Latina, or Asian women artists;

By Marcia Tucker

between women artists who felt a need to claim a different voice, equal to if not more valid than the dominant aesthetic, and those who felt that the most profound kinds of experience, those most suited to artistic exploration, were intrinsic to humanity and not gender-based.

Modernism, the artistic canon of the period, embodied the mainstream values of the culture at large and by its very nature was resistant to feminism. It virtually eliminated not only women but all artists of color. Modernism stresed the idea of the artist as a solitary genius, creating works of lasting value that existed outside time, history, or specific social site. It upheld the notion of a single standard of quality against which all works could objectively be measured and which was formed by a consensus of educated opinion, stemming largely from those who wished to perpetuate their own values. In the words of Paul Lauter, such a canon is "a means by which culture validates social power." While most men chose not to challenge the canon, due to their vested interest in it, many women who might have been in position to do so — including critics, curators, dealers, and the few female artists who were famous — instead largely adapted the methods and goals of the mainstream for the sake of visibility and success.

That so many women did not work actively toward social change was due in part to the fact that until the early 1970s there was no support system for them. The choice was either to join the "boy's club" or go their solitary ways. Women teachers in art schools and university art departments were rare, a situation that deprived younger women of much-needed role models. And it has always been simply more difficult for women to make art, because making art costs money and grants were — and still substantially are — more readily available to men.

Strange as it may seem today, women at that time were divided on the issue of whether discrimination itself even existed. Artists' comments on the topic, published in *Arts Magazine* in February 1971, ranged from one painter's statement that "as far as I am concerned, the problem of the sexes in art has never

existed, and if it still exists for some women painters, they must look into themselves for the reasons, not into the society that surrounds them," to Lee Krasner's tart response that "any woman artist who says there is no discrimination against women should have her face slapped."

By 1980 earlier differences had dissolved in a wave of optimism, and for a brief moment it seemed as though the battle had been won. Kay Larson, writing in *ARTnews*, credited "most of the interesting and important stylistic developments of the decade" to feminism. She asserted that "for the first time in Western art, women are leading, not following. And far from displacing men, female leadership has opened up new freedom for everyone." Women were touted as having pioneered the use of a subjective, personal voice; overtly political content; the diaristic mode; performance as autobiography; pattern and decoration; dream images, mythic and ritual practices in art; and the dissolution of differences between "low" and "high" art. Certainly it seemed as though women had defied the canon, rent the fabric of the mainstream, and provided new arenas of style and content. Unfortunately, too often it was the men who became famous, reaping the economic rewards of the changes wrought by women.

While women predominate in the museum profession at large, our numbers decrease as one looks higher in the ranks. Less than 5 percent of museum directors, for example, are women. Nor are women artists that much better off than they were in 1970. Unhappily, the statistics still tell much the same story in terms of museum exhibitions, gallery representation, sales, major articles, important grants and commissions, and tenured teaching positions.

Part of the reason that so little substantive change has taken place is that, once again, Americans are living in a politically conservative climate — one that in recent years has enabled the defeat of the Equal Rights Amendment, mobilized forcefully against women's control of our own bodies and the right to abortion, encouraged homophobia, responded to the AIDS epidemic by promoting heterosexuality and the traditional nuclear family as "natural," and in general nurtured a determined backlash to feminist attitudes and strategies.

By placing artistic concerns squarely in the context of the larger world rather than locating them in a supposedly objective art-historical narrative, artists and critics of the 1980s provided a broader theoretical approach to feminist issues. Like the analyses undertaken by Linda Nochlin a decade earlier, this approach actively engaged with other kinds of discourse, including the politics of the Left, new psychoanalytic investigations abroad, philosophical debates on the nature of postmodernist culture in general, and a large body of literary theory and criticism from France and England.

A great deal of recent feminist activity has consisted of attempts to locate art within a broader arena of theoretical discourse. We are asking questions about difference of all kinds: gender, race, age, sexual orientation, ethnicity. We are looking at works of art and asking questions about the nature of representation and how it conditions the way we identify ourselves and are identified to others. In terms of visual representations of all kinds, we want to know who is looking and who is being looked at. Increasingly we are seeing that the "self" is neither basic nor fixed but fluctuates according to where one is positioned and who is doing the positioning. Language, seen as a patriarchal construct into which we are all born and which predetermines our identities, is being deconstructed.

One of the earliest practical attempts to locate art within the arena of theoretical discourse was the 1983 exhibition entitled *The Revolutionary Power of Women's Laughter*, organized by Jo Anna Isaak. The show explored aspects of women's work that addressed not our exclusion from the world but our difference, our position as "Other." The exhibition provided an analysis of how meaning is constructed by focusing on specifically feminist strategies in the work while subverting gender identification. Much of the work for example, resisted stereotypical female-male identity by emphasizing instead the importance of the viewer's relationship to the image (whom is the image addressing, how, and why?); by proposing a self

that is neither basic nor fixed but constituted through images that re-present it; by seeing language as crucial in the formation of our identity; and by using images in a literal, unambiguous way as a deconstructive and ultimately subversive device. Changing the focus from women artists' marginalization to the underlying meaning of images themselves and that meaning can be reconstituted provided a very different vantage point for feminists. It eliminated much of the "male hating" stereotype previously used to denigrate feminists and substituted a more sophisticated theoretical approach that reverberated in the prevalent cultural and political discourse of postmodernism. Thus the debate centering on feminist issues, formerly seen as being of concern only to women, became potentially interesting to men as well and viable to an intellectual community at large.

By now the options open to women artists are certainly broader, although the terrain on which they are being exercised is no less hazardous. Rather than using imagery based on what has been thought of as specifically female experience — childbearing and rearing, domestic work, the iconography of physical and emotional differences — artists are now examining images, whether made as "originals" or taken from the media and transformed, for the ways in which meaning is constructed through visual representation in the culture at large. Today so-called female experience is construed by many feminists as culturally determined, and the concept of a uniquely female sensibility or female nature is considered an enforcement of stereotypes symptomatic of the political repression of women in general. What we think of as "natural" is generally whatever the culture is accustomed to and needs, and so the idea of a female "nature" supports the status quo even more profoundly than does the idea of female experience.

Similarly, the concept of absolute meaning in works of art supports the artistic canon's exclusivity: if a work has only one possible meaning, either you get it or you don't, and most people don't. But meaning today is construed as being situated both within the work itself and outside it, in the context in which it is presented and in the multiplicity of experiences and viewpoints brought to bear by those who see the work.

As for representation, woman, having been seen always as object rather than as subject, the viewed rather than the viewer, has been denied both subjectivity and power. Since our identity is formed by the ways in which we are represented in the world, that representation came to constitute "reality." Now this "reality" is being deconstructed and contested.

In recent years contemporary critical analysis has relied heavily on psychoanalytic studies, such as Jacques Lacan's radical rereading of Freud, in which traditional concepts of masculine and feminine are replaced by an understanding of sexuality in terms of the "active" or "passive" positioning of the subject. In Lacan's purposefully difficult writing, the multiplicity of meaning in a given text (or work of art) allows for a constantly shifting series of interpretations rather than to a single "correct" reading. In the same way, difference, rather than being a means of substituting one set of aesthetics or standards for another — women's for men's — is seen as a tool in the process of analysis and, ultimately, of change. It is the awareness of difference that prompts this kind of analysis in the first place.

The question of what constitutes feminist practice is still very much debated. The possibilities range from the use of critical and subversive elements in the making of work to questions of how to use a specifically feminist history (or art history) in attempting to rupture damaging and repressive cultural myths.

In some arts organizations, notably the very few that are run by feminist women, there is interest not merely in having more women represented in exhibitions or on the staff but in publicly examining the construction of gender through representation. We are concerned with seeing the museum and its exhibition and management practices as gendered spaces subject to critique and revision, like all other aspects of our lives in which issues of gender, race, and class play a role. Considering that in the past the only solid possibilities for women in museums lay in the roles of muse or nude, we've seen enormous progress.

But there is at present no agreement as to what constitutes feminism and no grounds for seeing women as an unalloyed force for good or as a unified sisterhood. We exist not in a simple polarity with males but in a complex, contradictory web of relationships and loyalties. There are as many feminisms as there are women and men involved in feminist issues.

Contemporary feminists' refutation of notions of an essential female nature and of a unified practice or ideology has encouraged tolerance — if not active support — of contradiction as an essential aspect of discourse. There is no single history or art history, no one attitude that all artists or artworkers hold in common, no defining vision of ourselves or of the context in which we live and work. Any history is determined by those who construct it as well as the purpose for which they do so, and each of us brings a different agenda to the construction and the telling.

Today, with the exception of a few individuals and an occasional group effort, such as that of the Guerrilla Girls, most feminist efforts are taking place in the arena of criticism and theory. Postmodernism has helped us think not in simple dichotomies of right and wrong, male and female, dominant and dominated, but in terms of discourse, the very nature of which precludes such polarization. We clearly need to think not about substituting women's power for men's but about how to examine, critique, and unsettle the very *concept* of power, and not just in terms of gender but of race and class as well. But we need to think *and* to act.

Such profound transformation is difficult and begins in many ways, from many places. What can we do? We can read, think, speak honestly, and listen to one another with respect for our differences; we can engage in critique and self-critique, individually and collectively; we can form coalitions, take action on the smallest to the largest levels, resist and resist again. We can and must act to ensure that feminist theory and practice meet in our own time.

This essay has been adapted from a lecture given by the author at l'École des Beaux Arts in Paris on March 23, 1990, and from the author's "Women Artists Today: Revolution or Regression?" in Randy Rosen and Catherine Brawer, compilers, *Making Their Mark: Women Artists Move into the Mainstream, 1970-85*, New York: Abbeville Press, 1989.

THE

*"In the first place, Cranford is in possession of the
Amazons."* —first line of Elizabeth Gaskells's *Cranford*

In the first place, we have "the." In Gaskell's 1851 novel
the narrator surmises that formidable Miss Jenkyns "would have
despised the modern idea of women being equal to men. Equal,
indeed! She knew they were superior"(17). Yet in the novel's
initial sentence a crucial "the" is missing before "possession," so
that it is Cranford town which owns the Amazons rather than
vice versa. With *The Revolutionary Power of Women's Laughter*,
we have "the" in the first place. Assertive "the" — a definite
article. Definite: to define, to set the limits.

What's In a Title?

There was a long moment when curator Jo Anna Isaak
thought to preface the title with "On," but was dissuaded from so
"uncertain" a beginning. Thus the choice of "the" revolutionary
power rather than "on the" revolutionary power or "a" or "this"
or "that" revolutionary power must also define the title's claims,
its own meaning-belief: perhaps that the laughter of all women is
revolutionary or that all laughter of any or all women is revolutionary. It invoked a unified front for one of the, if not "the"
first exhibition in a "mainstream" commercial New York gallery
to break the eerie silence cloaking the backlash against first-
wave feminist art of the '60s and '70s; for one of, if not "the,"
first such intent on making continental poststructuralist theory
respond to feminist art, a decisive power-seizing gesture
for January 1983, so close to Orwell's 1984. The proclama-
tory "the," like Barbara Kruger's accusatory and Jenny Holzer's
regulative language, should be seen in the context of
what Meagan Morris calls "the privilege trope of 1980s
entrepreneurial (or bull market) culture . . . 'the brutal truth' . . .

[that there is] no limit beyond which one cannot go . . . no
matter how predatory" (28). "The" fights fire with fire in the
same way that many '80s feminists appropriated the imagery of
a postindustrial landscape. Take Ilona Granet's *Bums/Bomb*, in
which the removal is twice effected: Granet's style in this piece
reflects that of superhero comix, themselves as heavily implicated
in and desperately struggling against the technological night-
mare as one of their protagonists, drawn to the honey pot of
some lethal vat of industrial accident and monstrously reborn
therefrom. Hung high over the entrance, these cartoons of a
landowner, industrialist, publisher, and general — all freak
spawn of early and high capitalism — occupied the position of
heroes but in their long semaphoric shape recalled banners in
meeting halls of the Reich. Curiously, the trembling line of

Granet's draftsmanship resisted the packaged gleam of those
seductive comix, asserting the presence of a hand, amateurish
or maybe just shaky with fear. This line was most unnerving, with
its contradiction of the sleekness otherwise invoked. It worried
one so, raising as it did the dreaded specter of an incompetent
woman, proving how thoroughly systematized expectations
had become. Being ideology, the aesthetic of smooth "pro-
fessionalism" (on the basis of which Reagan was declared to
have won his televised debate with Carter) was unconscious-
ly incorporated by all genders. In Granet's "imperfect" graphics
were the fault lines, the unbearable tension of a generation
of women artists whose "deviations," unlike their male coun-
terparts', would not be deemed expressive: to work out another
way without being an "other," knowing, in fact, one could
not be completely "other" even if one wished, that one's
mandated role as foil for and definer of "man" positioned one

By Jeanne Silverthorne

inside as well as outside the category of "human." The discomfort of *Bums/Bomb* provided an interesting light by which to view the unflappable "finish" of works by Kruger, Holzer, and Mary Kelly, and, if you will, may have revealed motivations less admitted to than those offered by Walter Benjamin for at least some decisions to array projects in the well-groomed glossiness of photography and typography.

Well, and so "the," defining, definite article, quite modest in this climate, drew its boundaries. One of these was a western perspective. How could it be otherwise? Asian speakers, for instance, learning English, often confuse "a" and "the," for their native languages require neither. The distinction between definite and indefinite articles is a peculiarity of many romance languages. Romance elicits "roman" or story, novel, meaning "new." Which brings us to "revolution." Is "revolution" itself embedded in western language?

This show indeed told a new story, but in order to make clear that it meant to be not just another new story — art history being nothing but new stories, the aim was to put feminist art in possession of the avant-gardo, not the avant-garde in possession of feminism — it borrowed the rhetoric of old art manifestoes: this was the new story, the revolution, but with a crucial addendum — "laughter," which word confiscated whatever factotum bombast might reside in "the." All was disrupted, undermined. This was a guerrilla war.

> "Truth's sacred Fort th' exploded laugh shall win."
> John Brown, *Essay on Satire*, 1715-66

And shall explode the fort to atomize "the" truth.

"The," a purely grammatical word — a mere marker — a word without definition in a sense but not without connotations: was this *the* feminist show of the '80s? To say that it was a feminist exhibition implies that there were many or even several, clearly not the case. Still, there were others, but they were not all perhaps visible to *the* art world. There are many art worlds in the art world but we all know which one is the art world.

But 1983 was not once upon a time; *The Revolutionary*

Power of Women's Laughter was not, is not, a fairy tale. It was a historical moment, the flavor of which might be captured by a mere listing of advertisements for shows in the major art magazines of the time. Here is a sample of the one-person exhibitions advertised for the same period as *The Revolutionary Power of Women's Laughter* in *Artforum* magazine: Richard Serra, Robert Rauschenberg, Tom Hatten, Barry Flanagan, Walter Murch, Marianne Stikas, David Amico, Jennifer Bartlett, Nancy Dwyer, Frank Faulkner, Fred Sandback, Tom Butter, Ian Carr-Harris, Bruce Parsons, Renée Van Halm, Ronnie Landfield,

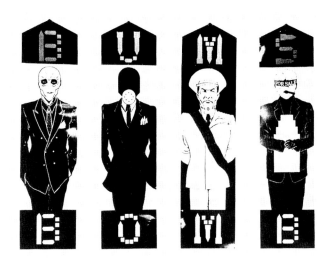

Ilona Granet

Roberto Juarez, Gerhard Richter, Robert Morris, Brian Eno, Bernard Faucon, Hervé deRosa, Jack Goldstein, Jackie Ferrara, Ellsworth Kelly, James Biederman, Ron Gorchov, David Salle, Jan Henle, Joan Mitchell, Richard Mock, Tom Otterness, Ron Cooper, Judy Pfaff, Eva Hesse, Gary Stephan, Thomas Nozkowski, Duane Michals, David Novros, Remo Salvadori, Joan Snyder, Robert Moskovitz, Cleve Gray, Sara Canright, Enzo Cucchi, Frank Lloyd Wright, William Schwedler, George

Baselitz, Jannis Kounellis, Loren Munk, Daniel Buren, John Albers, Gerard Garouste, Keith Haring, Robert Longo, Robert Ryman, Robert Racine, Martin Johnson, Milton Avery, Chambas, Ger van Elk, Stephen Chapin, Jody Mussoff, Eugene Brodsky, Louise Nevelson, Phil Sims, Frank Gillette, Janet Fish, Robert Kitchen, Lewis Baltz, Sam Messner, Judy Rifka, David Salle, Lois Lane, Yon Ringelhelm, Aldo Spoldi.

This was a period of massive reaction against the decorative artists of the late '70s, overwhelmingly women, whose very existence was wiped out in official '80s accounts of the art of the '70s, which tended to jump from postminimalism and conceptualism to the "return of painting," namely Neo-expressionist figuration. No notice was taken of how imagery had regained acceptance after so long a hegemony for abstraction and minimalism, of how "pure" form might have broken open under pressure of women's need to speak. The testimonial nature of early feminist work became "new image" and "naive nouveau," which paved the way for the rage for Neo-expressionism. Now, however, not only had German expressionism and Abstract Expressionism, the reference points for the new "wild style," been nearly entirely male, so were the contemporary Italian and German painters suddenly lionized by New York. Notions of "genius" returned and valorized a host of young male American painters as well. In fact, so virulent was the myth of uncontrollable creative male libido that the satirical productions of certain male painters, such as Mike Glier and Leon Golub, were insistently tagged Neo-expressionist in attempts to siphon off their criticality.

On the one hand, "the" suggests the one rather than the many — one feminism rather than feminisms; on the other hand, just as the word "definite" fissures into "de-finite," that is, "un-limit," so did the representations of feminism in the show multiply

and contradict. Not only did Isaak declare that the "feminist 'we' addressed by the exhibition . . . was not gender exclusive" but the new generation of artists who "utilized semiotic theory to address issues of sexual and historical determinism" met with an earlier generation in Nancy Spero, whose work had been doing this for some time. A bridge was thus shown to exist between the narrative thrust of earlier feminist work and the more recent and self-consciously language-based art. The customary ritual murder of anxiety-provoking parental influences was firmly rejected.

"The" may be more definite and thus exclusionary than "a," but one cannot use "a" before a plural noun as one can "the." "The," then, is open to and carries the capacity for plurality. And, indeed, this essay is occasioned by a second *The Revolutionary Power of Women's Laughter* (or is it the fourth, since the first had three slightly different incarnations in New York, Toronto, and Maryland) in which some of its definitions, frames, and limits have been rearranged.

With apologies, then, some memories of the opening of the first *The Revolutionary Power of Women's Laughter*.

There was no smell of fresh oil paint.

A spirit of contagious protectiveness erupted around Spero's scrolls; a wave or warnings to keep a clear space for the fragile paper oscillated along the edges of the crowd, a rare instance of custodial viewing.

The gallery was mobbed, but some of the work was "skied"; consequently, necks craned upward in the attitude necessary for viewing portraits of hero-workers, which seemed appropriate given the "socialist," agitprop presentation, with so many of the contributions unframed and sloganeering.

REVOLUTIONARY

Louis XVI: *"Is it a revolt?"*
Duc de la Rochefoucauld-Liancourt: *"No, Sire, it is a revolution."* —Spoken upon the arrival at Versaille of news of the fall of the Bastille, 1789.

How revolutionary can a gallery venue be?

"This exhibition has a noble purpose, and is, both visually and conceptually, brilliant. However . . . the attempt to use the art gallery as a political forum . . . is a leftism that goes no farther than the gallery — the art world. . . . It is a leftism calculated to make a certain impact, occupy a certain position in the art world" (Kuspit, 24).

This art did indeed aim to have an impact on the art world. Galleries in 1982 were still disproportionately male, as shown by Guerrilla Girl statistics from even later in the decade, and despite the by then high visibility of a handful of women, many of them showcased commercially in this prescient exhibition for the first time. As Rey Chow argues, specificity is the key to an activism that yet remains anti-essentialist, that acknowledges subjects with distinct predicaments but understands those contexts to be affected by time and circumstance. "The question that feminists must ask repeatedly is: how do we deal with the local?" (113). More than ten years later, the situation for women in the art world has changed considerably (although, if there is more room for women in the art world at the moment, one paranoid explanation is that there is little money at stake in this postrecessionary market). As for the end of sexism, it is with astonishment that one hears the now abhorrent decadence and selling-out of the '80s associated not with figures such as David Salle or Julian Schnabel but Barbara Kruger and Sherrie Levine. This is a mirror image of the charge that the Pattern and Decoration movement bankrupted the art world at the end of the '70s by reneging on its financial promise. Women's work was blamed for the economic collapse caused by rapacious appetites.

Today, the same charge of irrelevance is leveled against art addressed to racism and homophobia as if art institutions are and have always been fully integrated, enlightened paradises instead of places where one frequently preaches not to the converted but the convinced.

How did "revolutionary" function in *The Revolutionary Power of Women's Laughter*? As an adjective, therefore subject to a noun, in subordination, here, to "power." Subordinated, is it diminished? The supplement "y," a common way of turning a noun into an adjective, is reminiscent of the way diminutives are formed: Janey, Jacky. Is "power" always more stable than change, turning, re-volution, so close to re-volition, willing anew? How can "power" be more powerful than change, since, as Trinh T. Minh-ha says, the one thing you can count on is change? Yet the adjective is the modifier, i.e., it affects the noun, qualifies it, constrains it. "Change" checks and balances "power"? What we have, obviously, is a circulation, a codependency of power and change.

Just how revolutionary, how combative (not necessarily the same thing) were these works? How did they treat changing power?

Glier seems to have made it a *fait accompli*. Power had already changed hands. His were portraits of women well known in the art world — *Artforum* editor Ingrid Sischy, critic Lisa Liebman, artist Jenny Holzer, to mention just three — all laughing or calling or shouting or yodeling — aggressive, celebrant.

Granet agitated for change, using placards against implacable foes who wore their anality in front of them, like shields, the better to protect their rear; they were, after all, "bums." This very shieldlike impregnability, however, compressed them into the one-dimensionality of sitting ducks, easy targets in a shooting gallery. There was hope for change.

The binding of Kruger's female figures or static images by monolithic accusations is broken by the very fact of such charges. Some change — a cracking up, perhaps — had therefore occurred; more was demanded.

Mike Glier

man's world, her son's, in which she could only repeatedly wonder, "What have I done wrong?" As the only process-oriented piece in the exhibition, Kelly's undertaking did not describe or point to change; advocate, celebrate, or memorialize change. The narrator lived change, documented change, but changes that marked the reinforcement of the unvarying symbolic order, which document would then change received order only by being shown in the symbolic order of the gallery system.

As trope, war figured prominently in the show. Kruger's pieces were like interrogations in torture chambers: images of razor blades, slashed-out phrases, dissected figures cowering in *noir* shadow bars. Holzer's papers might have been dropped into enemy territory, only clearly meant to confuse the populace, subversive not of an enemy order but of order itself. There was the camouflage background of Glier's paintings, which oddly functioned to flush the women out, no longer in need of protective coloring (masquerade?). The harsh lines habitual to Glier's drawing style here increased the women's toughness. Like Spero's women, they suggested the Amazonian. Only Kelly's work appeared removed from war metaphors, although in this company she could be said to have functioned as reconnaissance or cryptographer — making and breaking codes. Paul Virilio distinguishes two aspects of our present state of "total war." He writes, "The drive is on for a general system of illumination that will allow everything to be seen and known in every moment and in every place" (4). Such surveillance was the method and target of Kruger and Kelly. Conversely, against the principle of weapons being publicized so as to have a real deterrent effect is the principle of "stealth" weapons, involved in "'the aesthetic of disappearance.'" Hence Holzer's use of building plaques, LED signs, leaflets to disguise her propaganda and Granet's use of street sign materials and codes to authorize her unofficial injunctions.

"I know and all the world knows that revolutions never go backward." — William Henry Seward, 1850

For Spero change was rendered as apocalyptic (she cites the *Beatus Apocalypse*, attributed to a 12th-century nun), already in place and finished. Her scrolls take an extremist stance — ranging from radical torture to radical joy — and strike a demonic, maenadic pose. That this is a pose, position, makes the idea of an end to struggle rhetorical, i.e., a particular kind of fiction that urges or incites to action, to change.

In the universe of Holzer's *Truisms* things had changed — certainly the center did not hold anymore — but not necessarily for the better. "In a way, the aphoristic precision and the commanding tone of her advice and injunctions remind me of the suggestion columns in women's magazines which . . . tell us how to achieve beauty, love, success, etc." (Handy, 56). A particularly new world kind of change — individual betterment, self-improvement, the will to perfection — is teased out and exhausted by her frustratingly contradictory messages.

Kelly noted changes in an unchanging sphere: it was a

"I have ever been of the opinion that revolutions are not to be evaded."
— Disraeli, *Coningsby*

How revolutionary can a second (or fourth) Revolutionary Power show be? Revolution need not be violent, of course, but there is rough force in the "re" that turns away from a quiet "evolution." It is the violence of repetition, always an unavoidable compulsion. There is no choice but to repeat, since to assume the "new" is to fall prey to the fallacy of the original. "We have only the poor freedom . . . to sign the pact that others have written for us" (Isaak). But "again" is never quite the same. We cannot repeat exactly; it is a nonidentical, discrepant repetition. And in that "never quite" and "not exactly" there is turning again, adjustment, tuning, change. Meanwhile, there is violence even in trying to re-member this first exhibition, a re-membering attempted through re-viewing the reviews.

POWER

"Four things greater than all things are —Women and Horses and Power and War"
— Kipling, *Ballad of the King's Jest*

Where are the horses?
Perhaps the titles have the horsepower to lead the charge. A selection: *Let the Priests Tremble* (Spero); *You molest from afar, Perfume is the charisma of your Gods* (Kruger); *Bums/Bomb* (Granet); *Action causes more trouble than thought, An elite is inevitable, Anger or hate can be a useful motivating force, Change is tolerable because it lets the oppressed be tyrants* (Holzer).
The power addressed and sought after in *The Revolutionary Power of Women's Laughter* resided in language, as curator Isaak made perfectly clear: "[This show] is an investigation of the ways in which we respond to and are constructed by language." Furthermore, words were treated as both targets and weapons,

capable of slipping from victim to aggressor. Power was thus courted, clasped, and contravened — undone in the very doing of it. Despite Holzer's self-subverted *Truism* that "ambivalence can ruin your life," an investigation of the inherent motility of power informed the attitude of the "word-smith" artists — Kruger, Kelly, Holzer, and Spero. Like Lacan's mirror, in which the infant, seeing itself separate, mistakes itself as whole, language teaches its users to comport themselves as subjects or objects, that is, as doers or receivers of action, to experience themselves as coherent over time, just as meaning inheres, is held together, during the passage of a sentence, paragraph, conversation. Yet, in giving us a sense of time, of memory which can posit future tense, language also imbues us with the foresight of our cessation. It provides the fiction of the self (fiction in the sense of constructed narrative, not falsehood) and of the dissolution of the self. And in giving us subject-object relations, it also undermines the very conviction of self-governance it is at pains to shore up. Kruger's work, in particular, made use of the fact that language consists of shifters, that one self's "you" is another self's "I," pronouns continually switching positions, uncertain as referents. In addition, unlikely as it seems now that we are in such complete possession of her stated intentions, it was possible for an early "uninformed" spectator to receive Kruger's ubiquitous "you" as an intimate "*tu*," to view the inscriptions as heterosexual or as lesbian love poetry, reminiscent at times of the sadomasochistic lament of Jean Rhys: "I am your slice of Life." At any rate, Kruger's subject, like Holzer's iconoclastic rule-bound one, took pleasure in binding and release. As Therese Liechtenstein wrote in an early review, "The splitting of her image . . . wounds the woman while it also refuses the wound, by recognizing conflict and despair"(4). The figure in one of the phototexts included in the exhibition stands in the frontal, hieratic pose of Lucas Cranach's *Lucretia*, bandaged by strips of phrases not unlike the gauzy length that veils and yet reveals Lucretia's privates, presenting the body as both dissected and mended by language. Whereas Lucretia aims the dagger at herself, Kruger's subject aims the stiletto/stylus/pen at "you," "you" being whoever does not identify with the speaker. Looking over a selection of her work circa 1983, we see that Kruger's male images from this period are often one-eyed or four-eyed, bespectacled or aided by ocular devices, medical ones sometimes, that should allow them to probe, to see better, but instead hint at a visual impairment with overtones of Oedipal or Cyclopean blinding. There is a reciprocity of blows between male and female. In *You molest from afar*, the shadowy male (?) figure could as likely be shielding his eyes from the light of inquiry as raising an arm to strike, and the bandaged, wounded hand in *We will undo you* reads as "masculine." There is even reciprocity between woman and woman — note the bullet-shattered mirror in *You are not yourself*. Ultimately this parity of blows has perhaps unequal effect but the exchange continues unimpeded: while the "scientist" in *Your fact is stranger than fiction* remains on top, literally and figuratively, and the men in *You molest from afar* and *Surveillance is your busywork* might at best seem only to flinch overseeing dismembered women, the stone head of *Your gaze hits the side of my face* leads logically past the petrification of the woman's visage to the shattering of the male "gaze" against her impervious cheek.

Medusa's echo presided over the exhibition to the extent that Cixous's famous phrase makes Medusa the link between women and laughter. Physically faced off in the gallery, Granet's shielded men played Perseus to Glier's laughing women, who are poised between climatic release and grimacing rictus. But it is Granet's officials who are petrified and decapitated, their faces transfigured as skulls, masked with blindfolds or aspirators, the crime appropriately redounding back to the criminals. For, as Lacan points out, how could Perseus cut off Medusa's head if she were already turned to stone? Surely the murderous capacity of Medusa's severe (severing) look must be a false "myth" fabricated to cover up the slaying of a living being. The shield then protects only in reflecting Perseus's fears. Freud saw castration anxiety in the myth; Cixous saw Freud projecting. Medusa, she claimed, could be seen head on, and she was beautiful and laughing. Perhaps the mirror of the shield performed not the usual left/right reversal but an up/down

inversion which put the devouring vagina where the openmouthed laugh had been — a displacement to disguise the fact that it is really women's mouths, their wit and ridicule, that are so fearsome.

Craig Owens judged the freezing action of the Perseus shield as proto-photographic, suturing up a moment of seeing with a moment of arrest — an interpretation which hooks back into feminist use of photography (101). This elision of seeing and arrest is also the labor of the fetish, which "freezes" on the object — shoe, undergarment — viewed just prior to the glimpse of the difference allegedly apprehended as loss. Mary Kelly fetishized the carefully preserved diapers, scribbling, etc., of her *Post-Partum Document*, evidence of separation that, in their keepsake capacity, denied the loss. Again, power percolates, ebbs, and flows. Kelly's dossier recorded cumulative loss building to a threshold of decisive parting, but it is a record of her child's successive masteries — his first words, his first solid foods — which, willy nilly, were also hers, and that record indicates a double mastery in another sense, since the fetish has been generally deemed a masculine formation. In addition, to supplant the "depression" which normally follows "post-partum" with "document" is to switch the roles of patient and doctor/scientist, which that classic "document" of post-partum depression, Charlotte Perkins Gilman's *The Yellow Wallpaper*, had so thoroughly exposed as those of prisoner and warden. But it is also, wittily, to conflate the two, so that Kelly becomes the "mad scientist." Instead of Nathaniel Hawthorne's insane Aylmer removing the birthmark of his wife, we have Kelly marking the birth of her son. If Holzer is Emily Dickinson out of retirement and gone into advertising, offering great bargains on cheap wisdom, Kelly is at once that bored housewife Madame Bovary, obsessed with a man, trying to turn the dross of quotidian drudgery into the gold of romance, and Gustave Flaubert, the dispassionate anatomist/observer. She knows that language — naming, writing — is power, for her son's signing of his own name is the culmination of his development, the passport of his parturition, the instituted proclamation of his difference from her.

Yet she has arranged matters so that every time her son, Kelly, signs his first name he simultaneously signs her last one. Thus the male Kelly, in writing, is read.

The detached tone of Kelly's and Holzer's writing provided a certain protection against their readers reading them. To some extent, this detachment also characterized the language of Kruger and Spero. But the removal, in Kruger's case, comes from an Olympian perspective of judgment which invites reaction. And, faced with the powerful imagery of birthing and quadruple-teated women in Spero's work, viewers could overlook its fictionality, its constructedness, in the same way that naive readers confuse narrator with author. In fact, not only does literature inform Spero's choices; ambiguity saturates them. One has only to glance at her *Codex Artaud* from the 1970s — Artaud, that hater of women and saint of artists — to see that she too was involved in the affairs of split consciousness. Her indexical method — cataloguing, listing — is one of the hallmarks of postmodernism. Nevertheless, Spero's enterprise, while one of quotation, is not appropriation precisely because she puts in the quotation marks — a signature style of uneven type, variegated in scale and face, and glyphic figures, although this is a "treehand" reined in by the use of stamps for the making of marks. Her scrolls "trickle through history and linguistics, through mythology, through polemic, through the records of barbarisms . . . [through] classical Greek and ancient Sumerian relics" (Liebman, 94-95). Mainly this was an archaeological undertaking, concerned with the business of ruins and therefore allegorical. That allegory, in the hands of '80s theorists, was such a vexed question — was it reactionary nostalgia or Borgesian palimpsest? — indicates the daunting nature of such an address at the time.

OF

"Of" does at least two things:

1. It generates, being a genitive. A generator, what does this "of" produce, make happen? Laughter. "Power" generates ("of") "laughter"; power makes for women's laughter. Women find power funny?

2. It objectifies. "Of," as pre-position, takes an object, which in the title is "women's laughter."

So power generates women's laughter and, conversely, power makes an object of women's laughter, makes it an "other." In the etymological soup, women's laughter became hysteria (of the womb), requiring regulation, institutionalization — and hysteria made women themselves objects whereby their wombs (hyster) became their all, part for whole, an unpleasant metonymy.

Of the artists in the show, only three directly depicted bodies. Writing about the empty spaces between events in Spero's scrolls, i.e., between bodies and words, critic Donald Kuspit opined that they were "horizonless voids of space . . . with all the dread they evoked" and connected them to the womb, which had become a "wasteland in which tenacious weeds grow — words and monstrously militant . . . figures." The womb is all-encompassing, the ground for monsters and weeds; the womb is empty, between events. In this poetic construal, whether perlieu or abyss, the womb is displaced, detached, ostracized.

Spero's products could seem most tied to the body simply because the human being is often figured there as beast — the she-wolf mother of Romulus and Remus, for example — pawing, prowling, and prancing through the space/time continuum. Her particular combination of word and image reinforces this sense if "the interruption of 'linear' writing by drawing, spatiality, volumetrics, may also be a moment of breach that is inevitably sexual (the imprint of the body or shape upon the clean page)" (Ingraham, 258). Nevertheless, her horizontal format offers the famous flat bed of the picture plane to leaping, jumping female figures who will not play the odalisque, who will not lie down.

"Of" — belonging to — the body possessed and possessing. In fact, bodies were the object of operations — grammatical and otherwise — in all the works in the exhibition, and some of these were male. Granet's closeted, coffined "gentlemen" (literally taken in part from *Gentleman's Quarterly*) were "quartered" in their bombs, like pharaohs, true, with the fragrance of power still clinging to them, but also costively, nonfunctional. In an odd way they became "feminized," not merely through their dandified appearance. After all, Granet's phallic bombs are "'unveiled' penile display [which] is . . . something less than phallic" (Morris, 9). (Cf. the interesting "effeminateness" of some male self-exposure performances.) In their cosseted stringency, the mannequins are as rigid as corpses, heroes of state, in glass cases. It's as if Granet were saying, "Let's put you in the double bind of powerlessness and repugnance."

The bomb bodies of Granet are virtually all body, and the body is virtually all machine. This contrasts with Glier's heads-without-bodies — as if he conscientiously wished to

avoid the whole problem. (They are alike, though, in that if Granet's gentlemen are bums, Glier's women are no ladies.) In line with Glier's caution was Kelly's publicized refusal to represent women's bodies. But, like Granet, she does limn in a male body. In fact, the *Document* might be said to remind men of their bodies, once completely dependent, food and excrement their all.

Throughout Jane Austen's novels, women characters are imbricated with the imagery of constriction. In Kruger's figures language binds, but they are also posed, they are stereotypes, another kind of binding, one that connects glamor to its origin in "spell" — to cast a glamor over. To the extent that Holzer's exhortations also constitute adherence to a stereotype (Isaak wrote that the *Inflammatory Essays* and *Truisms* "arrest the consumer of language in the act of conformity"), her otherwise absent figures are also spellbound — literally en-chanted, litanized into "normality." As a result, the flitted but conjured body in Holzer's world is all mouth. Orality rules. Holzer characterized the lips as compelling because it's where the "slippery inside meets the dry outside." One of the things that slips out is laughter — the laughter that accompanies Lewis

Carroll's slide through the hole on the surface of language, kept as surface by ignoring — as Holzer does — its claim to truth value.

WOMEN'S

The apostrophe here indicates ownership, but this mark of self-possession is really a mark of contraction since "women's" was originally "women his," just as "the boy's coat" was once "the boy his coat." The history of language and law coincide; women air their property rights in a posthumous legality.

LAUGHTER

"The horn, the horn, the lusty horn
Is not a thing to laugh to scorn."　　　 *– As You Like It*

"In my mind, there is nothing so illiberal and so ill-bred as
audible laughter."　　　 – Earl of Chesterfield

Why is it that the author of a witticism does not laugh? The psychoanalytic explanation is that too much energy is needed to overcome the prohibition of the reality principle against play. For the auditors, on the other hand, the jester having done this work for them, the same energy is discharged in a hoot, a howl, a snort.

What other inhibitions did the artists of *The Revolutionary Power of Women's Laughter* overcome to produce laughter? And, if the artists did not laugh themselves, then who were the women laughing in the title?

If the revolutionary laughter was that of the women of the audience, it was still an art world audience. Some of the chuckles were the relief of hearing that the emperor had no clothes. In other words, much of what these revolutionary artists poked fun at was art discourse itself. No doubt a history of women's art could be written as a compilation of iconoclastic satire on the Great Tradition. That, for instance, one of the most definitive gestures of the '70s was Ree Morton's and Cynthia Carlson's bake sale response to an otherwise male faculty exhibition — cakes and stand — complete with the decorative vocabulary of swags, bows, swirls, and rosettes characteristic of their subsequent gallery production — is not perhaps so anomalous as would first appear.

Richard Armstrong claimed that Holzer's "distillations" let "the last of the air out of the work of Joseph Kosuth and company" (76). Indeed, they oxygenated the private, solipsistic performances recommended by Alan Kaprow, literally taking pearls of contemplation out of the head and, in a parody of the Barbizon exodus from the dark studio, into the *plein air* of the city street. Kruger, as did all the artists in the show, attacked the "aura" of the art work, equating it with "charisma," "the perfume of your Gods," and, through perfume's connection to commodity and "feminine" seduction, exposed the homology of sexism and connoisseurship. Kelly's *Document* was, in effect, a parody of conceptual documentation — instead of photos of mounds of moved dirt, photos of dirtied diapers, moved bowels. The document was also the solution to a dilemma: how can a woman be an artist when she is stuck at home with a baby? Again, it adopted the mode of Kaprow's mental performances, the turning of daily tedium into meditative art. At the same time, it shed light on the blind spot of such programs — the presumption that a busy mother or any busy worker would have the leisure for such cognitive gymnastics. Kelly might be said to have spoken up for Xanthippe, who, banished, was as absent from the obsessively philosophized death of Socrates as were mentions of his physical body. Glier's women were all art-world habituées, perhaps laughing their heads off but maybe heckling: get that comedian off the stage. Apparently, they didn't find his patter amusing any more. Spero's humor was scatological, carnivalesque — "we will show them our sects"; in its willing exposure to physical damage it thumbs its nose at archival preciosity. Granet's targets are slapstick, the humor of the pie in the face, the pleasure of "ducking" people at a fair.

Perhaps laughter, being a kind of nonsense talk, is related to Kristeva's notion of the semiotic, which "disrupts signifying process[es] through . . . mere sound," among other methods. If Kristeva's assertion that the semiotic "indicates maternal drives . . . which characterize the dependency of the infant's body" seems too essentializing, that problem was neatly sidestepped by the replacement of guffaw with wit in *The Revolutionary*

Nancy Spero

Power of Women's Laughter. Holzer, for instance, wedges Kristeva's multivocality into the monolith of univocal symbolic power, but makes nonsense of the master discourse by mimicking its tone of cultural legitimacy. Isaak made an implicit connection between laughter and language (rather than nonsense), titling the show to indicate its subject as laughter but declaring in her commentary that the topic was language: "The aim is both to dismantle the presumption of the 'innocence' of the signifying system and to explore the only signifying strategy which allows the speaking subject to shift the limits of its enclosure — through play, *jouissance*, laughter." When laughter and language meet, we have wit. And wit is the place where the anarchic — wit in its relation to the unconscious — and the elegant meet.

Bums, guns, puns.

"They laugh that win."   – Othello

Works Consulted

Armstrong, Richard. Review. *Artforum*, February 1984, 76.

Chow, Rey. "Postmodern Automatons," in Butler, Judith, and
    Joan W. Scott, eds., *Feminists Theorize the Political*. New York
    and London: Routledge, 1992.

Foster, Hal. "Subversive Signs." *Art in America*, November 1982,
    88-92.

Gaskell, Elizabeth. *Cranford*. 1851.

Handy, Ellen. Review. *Arts*, January 1984, 56.

Ingraham, Catherine. "Initial Proprieties: Architecture and the Space
    of the Line," in Colomina, Beatriz, ed., *Sexuality and Space*.
    Princeton: Princeton Architectural Press, 1992.

Isaak, Jo Anna. Catalogue essay and press release for *The Revolutionary
    Power of Women's Laughter*. New York: Protetch McNeil, 1983.

Kristeva, Julia. *Desire in Language: A Semiotic Approach to Literature
    and Art*. New York: Columbia Univ. Press, 1980.

Kuspit, Donald. "Gallery Leftism." *Vanguard*, November 1983, 22-25.

    "From Existence to Essence: Nancy Spero." *Art in America*, January
    1984, 88-96.

Lichtenstein, Therese. Review. *Arts*, May 1983, 4.

Liebman, Lisa. Review. *Artforum*, March 1984, 94-95.

Morris, Meaghan. "Great Moments in Social Climbing: King Kong and
    the Human Fly," in Colomina, Beatriz, ed. *Sexuality and Space*.
    Princeton: Princeton Architectural Press, 1992.

Owens, Craig. "The Medusa Effect, Or, the Spectacular Ruse." *Art in
    America*, January 1984, 97-106.

Spivak, Gayatri Chakravorty. "French Feminism Revisited: Ethics and
    Politics," in Butler, Judith, and Joan W. Scott, eds., *Feminists
    Theorize the Political*. New York and London: Routledge, 1992.

Virilio, Paul. and Sylverre Lotringer. *Pure War. Semiotext(e)* 4, 1992.

Essays on the Artists

By Jo Anna Isaak

All looking involves risk — to the voyeur as well as to the person or object of the gaze. Part of the pleasure in scopophilia is derived from the threat or guilt involved in looking at what is culturally taboo. Dotty Attie is an artist who isn't afraid of visual pleasure. She takes the viewer into the operating amphitheater of art history and seduces us into watching, in sensual slow motion, the anatomy of a murder.

For over twenty years — in tiny, usually no more than six-inch-square canvases — Attie has been engaging in a detailed pictorial exegesis of the meta-narratives of art history. The paintings she dissects are all well known to us: part of our visual history, images already seen within in this culture. We recognize that bloody hand holding the scalpel from Eakins's *Gross Clinic*, the sensuous commingling of flesh and fabric from Ingres's *Turkish Bath*, those manacled limp arms from *Roger Rescuing Angelica*, the erect nipple protruding through the fingers of Cupid as they clasp Venus's breast from the great Bronzino *Allegory*. Attie, like the painters she copies, is a realist, which, as Roland Barthes explains, is not to copy reality but to pastiche things already given within a culture, "to unroll the carpet of the codes." Attie unrolls the codes very slowly, freeze-frame by freeze-frame, heightening the significance of the fragments, increasing the erotic charge of the intersection of bodies and fabric, making the process of viewing more sensual and the viewer more conscious of the act of viewing.

Attie is not a closet copyist. Like Bertolt Brecht, who when accused of plagiarism berated himself for being only a petty thief when what he really aspired to be was a great criminal like Shakespeare, Attie is a flagrant and promiscuous copier. Unlike most subversive appropriationists who rephotograph reproductions of well-known works of art, Attie repaints them, reduplicating not just the image but the act of creation itself. She reenacts the painstaking pleasure to be had from the sensuous, viscous quality of oil paint, the rich shine of the colors, the repetitive, caressing activity of the brush, the delight in engendering the images in the first place.

In the *After Courbet* series (1993) Attie looks directly at the source of the problem of representation. Using that ur-text of representation, Courbet's *The Origin of the World*, she explores the latent motive behind all realist painting: the desire to know our origin. Courbet's painting was commissioned by a Turkish diplomat. "An elegant gentleman, cultivated and artistically knowledgeable came to his studio with an unusual commission . . . his sense of delicacy made a direct explanation difficult." The painting was intended for his private delectation: But all this discretion surrounding the painting was violated when the diplomat went bankrupt and the painting was exhibited for public sale. The painting went missing for many years and was found again in Jacques Lacan's country house. Each owner of *The Origin of the World* was moved by a sense of decorum to

Dotty Attie

conceal the painting in some way. At one time it was covered by a sliding panel representing a castle in the snow. When in Lacan's possession, it was concealed by an elaborate wooden device made by André Masson, representing in abstract the hidden painting. Clearly, knowledge of the "lack" as Lacan would put it, needs to be kept a secret or revealed to only a select few. Understanding this castration anxiety, Attie covers the female genitals with other images — that bloody hand holding the scalpel or a self-portrait of Courbet looking as horrified as if he had just glimpsed the void with his own eyes.

Dotty Attie was born in 1939 in Pennsauken, New Jersey, and received an M.F.A. from the Philadelphia College of Art. Her work was shown in the Corcoran Biennial in 1994 and in *Going for Baroque* at the Walters Art Gallery in Baltimore in 1995. She lives and works in New York City.

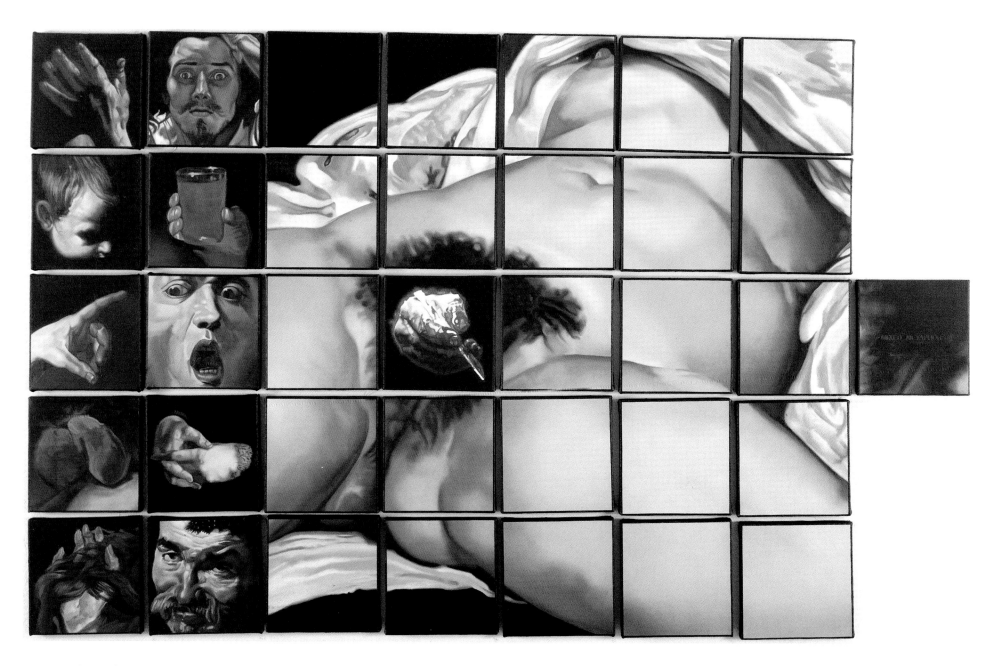

Mixed Metaphors 1993

Marie Baronnet's work suggests that the female body has the potential to break the stereotypes into which images of that body have been forced. Using a black background, a Polaroid camera with a timer, and her own nude body, Baronnet achieves one of the principle objectives of the feminist movement: the reclamation of the image of woman from the representations of others.

Like Cindy Sherman, Baronnet uses her own body to "ruin" representations of women, but unlike Sherman she does away with the masquerade of femininity. All the accoutrements of the feminine struggle to conform to a facade of desirability — cosmetics, wigs, high heels, even clothes — are removed. Baronnet presents her naked form in the simplest way, without props, without any artificial influences altering the appearance. Most important, she does not assume the pose of femininity — the erotic, suggestive poses in which the woman is usually placed to connote sexuality.

The photographs reiterate the "to-be-looked-at-ness" of femininity in parodic form. They make the feminine visible, so visible, in fact, that it is almost unrecognizable. At first glance the images seem to be antic parsnips photographed by Edward Weston rather than a series of photographs of a woman. Their fascination is derived from their quality as trompe l'oeil. The viewer is subjected to a series of double takes, estrangements, and recognitions that throw a monkey wrench into the mechanism of the gaze. In response to the pornographic demand to "Take it off!" she complies completely; she is the girl who goes too far. The striptease fails precisely because she unveils too much, revealing that the nude in photography, the perfect body produced by the apparatus of photography, is a defense against just such an anxiety-provoking, uneasy, and uncanny body. She reveals that the masquerade of femininity has been donned by women in order to spare the male psyche the discomfort of having to confront the physicality of the female body, of having to recognize sexual difference.

Flamboyantly exhibitionistic, free to assume any and every position no matter how unseductive, how indecorous, *this woman makes a spectacle of herself*. This is the female figure *en liberté*, going through a series of metamorphoses, shaping a new language of femininity. With her own body, Baronnet is writing the hierogyphics of a new speech.

Marie Baronnet was born in 1972 in Paris. She currently attends l'École des Beaux-Arts. She has exhibited at Gallerie Pascale Lesnes in Paris and Galerie Fiction in Tokyo.

Marie Baronnet

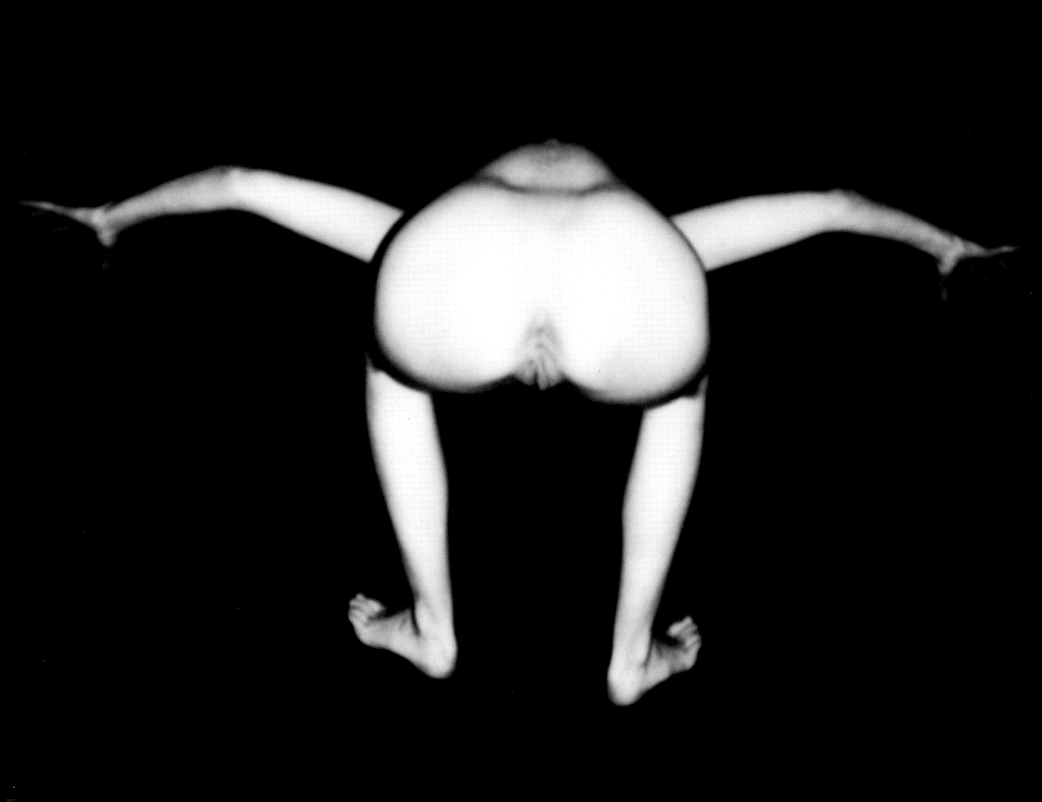

Dorothy Cross

The chauvinist and colonizing impetus of mapping is revealed by Dorothy Cross, one of a number of Irish women artists who have adopted a subversively humorous approach to the "troubles" in Ireland. Cross sculpted two bronze maps — one of Ireland and one of England — to serve as latrines and installed them in a derelict Victorian men's public underground toilet in the East End of London. The reopening of this public convenience, which had long stood idle, was Cross's contribution to *Edge '92*, an international biennale of innovative visual art that took place in the economically and racially mixed neighborhood of Spitalfields. Cross's site-specific installation is an interactive art work: as with all public toilets, a choice must be made before you enter, but in this case the signs over the doorway do not discriminate along the usual gender lines. Instead they read "IRISH" and "ENGLISH." The signs recall the 19th-century British mapping of Ireland and the Anglicizing of Irish place names as well as the American practice of using "COLORED" signs on public toilets or publishing help-wanted ads with qualifications such as "No Irish, Jews, or Italians need apply." The work is also a reminder of the fact that the job of attendant in public latrines in England was often occupied by Irish immigrants.

Ironically, or perhaps inevitably, as with all such neat divisions, these signs lead you astray, as either choice leads to the main toilet area. On the wall, hanging where the Victorian loos have been removed, are the two bronze urinal/map sculptures. The participant/patron can both assert a national identity and lay claim to another country in the simple and satisfying manner of a dog staking out his territory. Once again, however, the choice offered is illusory, for whether one chooses to relieve himself in the basin shaped like Ireland or the one shaped like Britain, the drain pipes protruding from the bottom of the bowls (which are cast in the shape of penises) point toward each other in such a way as to pun, in good Joycean fashion, upon the meaning of "the meeting of the waters." Working on that age-old presumption that man is the measure of all things, Cross settles the "troubles" by making the penises on Ireland and Britian the same size.

Dorothy Cross was born in Cork, Ireland, in 1956. She received a B.A. from Leicester Polytechnic in England and an M.F.A from the San Francisco Art Institute. She was Ireland's representative in the 1993 Venice Biennale. She now lives in Dublin.

Nancy Davidson

In the contemporary concern about rabid consumerism, we are dealing not just with consumption, but with consumption conceived as a threat, particularly with the unlicensed appetites of women, for it is women who are placed in the role of preeminent consumers. This is the modern-day equivalent of the gargantuan appetites described by Rabelais — the unlicensed, potentially engulfing appetites of the material bodily principle. Although contemporary mass culture may be a long way away from the popular culture of Rabelais's day, both derive their identity in part from the pejorative characteristics attributed to them, characteristics historically thought of as feminine. Baudrillard uses the term "engulfment" in describing what he sees as the radical potential of rabid consumerism: "a system is abolished only by pushing it into the hyperlogic . . . . You want us to consume — O.K. let's consume always more, and anything whatsoever, for any useless and absurd purpose."

Nancy Davidson's inflatables (gargantuan weather balloons over six feet in diameter) take over the exhibition space, threatening to engulf the viewer. Excess, positive exaggeration, eroticism, hyperbole, transgression are what the work is about, particularly the grotesque's ability to transgress even its own body. Like a clown at the carnival, Davidson presents the audience with balloons large enough to fulfill our childhood desire for the biggest one. Each balloon is dressed in a tutu with fetishistic straps that bifurcate it into the two halves of a grotesquely fat derriere floating, lighter than air, up to the ceiling where it "moons" the spectator.

Wearing their underwear as outerwear, these material girls with untrammelled appetites explore the comic excess at the intersection of exaggeration and eroticism, the subversive potential of what anthropologist Victor Turner rather deliciously describes as "the carnivalized feminine principle." They are part of the disruptive excess of feminist intervention in the production and consumption of art. The danger here is not simply female "unruliness," but that the sense of the ridiculous which informs the work's art-historical critique may not be kept in check. This unruliness itself is the mark of the ultraliminal, of the perilous possibility of "anything goes," which threatens any social order. While pop art brought mass culture "up" into the realm of high art, these daughters of Niki de Saint Phalle and Claes Oldenburg traffic in a two-way street, inviting intercourse with the politically as well as the aesthetically marginalized.

Nancy Davidson was born in Chicago in 1943. She received her B.A. from the University of Illinois at Chicago and an M.A. from the School of the Art Institute of Chicago. Recent exhibitions include "No End To Her," Richard Anderson Gallery, NYC; "Maux Faux," Ronald Feldman Gallery, NYC; and "Bad Girls West," UCLA, Los Angeles. She now lives and works in New York City.

Nancy Dwyer

"Words are a plastic material with which one can do all kinds of things."
— Freud, "Jokes and Their Relation to the Unconscious."

As if taking the plasticity of words literally, Nancy Dwyer makes language laugh by making it concrete, giving words a physical presence appropriate to their meaning. Words are the subject and substance of her sculptures and graphic paintings. Rather than mapping words onto a body, she gives them bodies of their own, which they occupy with a "presence" appropriate to their power and privilege. In *Big Ego* (1990) the word EGO is made of huge yellow air-filled balloons that take up all the available space in the room. While the words are bigger than the spectator, their fragility is apparent in that they are continually deflating and in need of being pumped up.

In a series of paintings of large maps of the United States, Dwyer explores the effects of language on the landscape. Viewed from the side, the maps are elongated by perspective and appear to be gigantic three-dimensional objects floating in space, something like the Starship Enterprise. Words are superimposed or intrude upon the maps. In one, the words "YOUR NAME HERE" are printed over the map and extend beyond its boundaries. The words echo the concrete poetry of the corporate logo found on billboard advertisements, but rather than being a brief intrusion on the landscape, this advertisement with its encircling logo seems to be the ultimate in manifest destiny, completely covering the continent. Other words, both violent and void, appear on similar maps, inscribing them differently and creating a different effect upon the map. The words "DAMN NATION WOMAN "are printed in red letters across the continental USA. They appear to be carved out of its three-dimensional structure, demarcating numerous deep chasms, and have cut holes right through the map as if in illustration of Irigaray's argument that woman is the *hole* in men's signifying economy.

Nancy Dwyer was born in New York City in 1954. She received a B.F.A. from the State University of New York at Buffalo. Her public sculptures can be seen in Cleveland and at the Criminal Justice Center in Philadelphia. She lives and works in New York City.

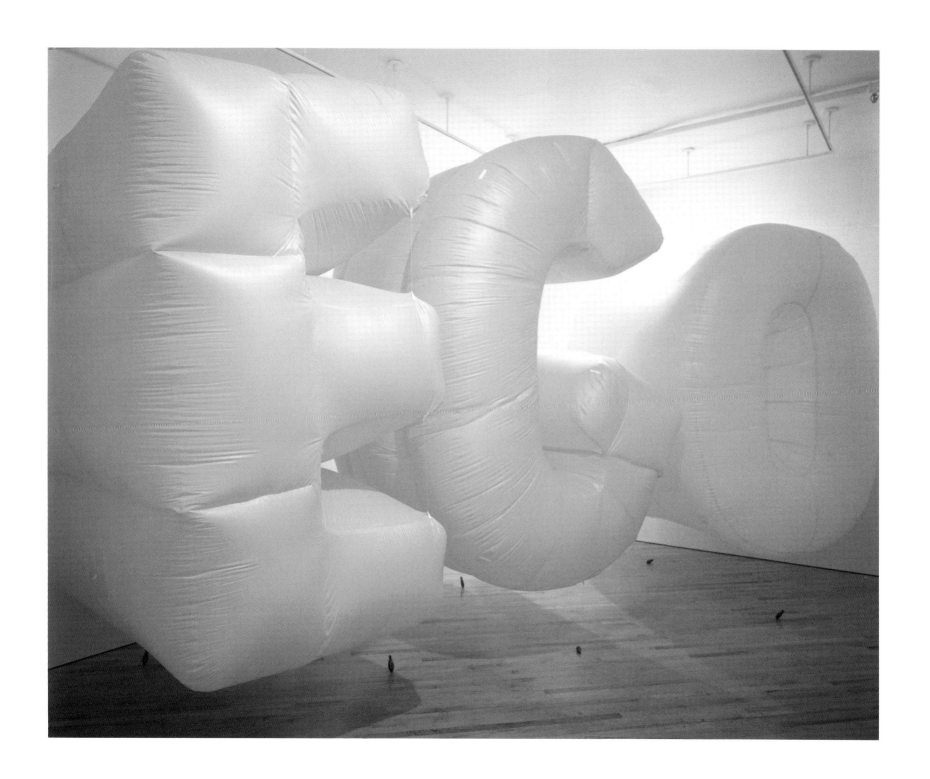

The area of common ground with postmodernism for a number of women artists is the marketplace of mass culture. While Tania Modleski cautions that women are victimized in many and complex ways by mass culture, a good number of contemporary women artists have nonetheless selected this as the site of their intervention. Jenny Holzer, Barbara Kruger, and Ilona Granet were among the first artists to occupy a terrain from which women had historically been excluded or negatively inscribed, or, if they entered, existed "at risk."

Ilona Granet began working, not in the studio, but in the market place of mass culture. She made her living as a sign painter; her work was to be found "skied" on billboards and buildings around the city of New York. She, like all sign painters, worked from a prescribed text, *The Sign Painter's Dictionary of Signs*, in which the agitprop symbols of heroic capitalism that surround us daily are reduced and standardized by a committee of cryptographers expert in inducing quick recognition and appropriate desire in the harried passerby. Her job was to arrest the attention of people who, as she says, "don't want to stop, don't want to read . . . it's all about no time and that's it."

For *The Revolutionary Power of Women's Laughter* exhibition Granet made signs of male authority figures. *Bums/Bomb* is four monolithic figures made from a collection of codes by which male success and male power are conveyed by this culture's system of signs. These superhero cartoons of a landowner, an industrialist, a media monopolizer, and a military leader are, Granet explains, "what I'm supposed to be advertising." (One of her employers was the media mogul Malcolm Forbes — she painted the name on his yacht.) These corporate warriors of high capitalism were encased in two huge sarcophagus-like missiles, "stealth weapons" in the "total war" of surveillance and control: "These guys are really comfortable in that space, aren't they? I mean, other figures, if you put them between two missiles, wouldn't look so relaxed." Appropriately, they were hung high over the entranceway to the exhibition. Their long semaphoric shape, Jeanne Silverthorne suggests, recall banners in meeting halls of the Third Reich. But here in the site of the carnival they are uncrowned and transformed into "funny monsters" to be dunked, the melancholy clowns of pie-throwing contests.

Granet is still working in the streets, trying to make them a bit more tolerable for women. In 1986 she became infamous for her *Emily Post Street Signs*, "regulations" for etiquette in public places. The injunctions are written in English and Spanish: "No cat calls, whistling and kissing noises" or "Curb your animal instincts." The image on the latter sign is of a beast straining on a leash toward a woman. Her work raises the obvious point that if there is a city ordinance against dog shit and horn blowing, why isn't there one against harassing women in the streets?

Ilona Granet

Ilona Granet was born in 1948 in Brooklyn, N.Y. She received a B.F.A. from Tyler School of Art and an M.F.A. from the School of the Art Institute of Chicago. In 1989 she received the Susan B. Anthony award from the National Organization for Women. She now lives and works in New York City.

Curb Your Animal Instincts   1986

Adapting Magritte's strategy of questioning representation in *This is Not a Pipe* to Lacan's famous formulation "The woman does not exist," Kathy Grove solves the problem by removing the question, that is, the woman. She rephotographs the canonical paintings and photographs of Western art and eliminates the female figure, making Magritte's play upon the pipe seem like a pipe-dream. There is more at stake in representation than the presence or absence of a pipe: we know that any challenge to

Kathy Grove

the image's power of illusion and address must simultaneously engage the question of sexual difference. Pipes are, after all, something of a rarity in art; the image of woman, on the other hand, is the traditional nodal point for the conceptualization of Man, Truth, History, and Meaning. Removing her confronts us with a very large *lacuna*. Without the imagined site of plenitude provided by the woman's body, the entire history of art changes: landscape painting reveals the pathetic fallacy we always projected onto nature; sheep lose their legitimating role as signifiers of the pastoral convention and take on the prurient interest that had once been focused upon the naked nymphs. Without some remnant of a woman, abstract expressionism occurs too early and too often, mythical and biblical genres are forced to change their stories. Paris still proffers that divisive apple, but now only the horse seems interested in it; family structures everywhere collapse; and so many, many beds are empty and unmade. . . Representation can't live with the woman-who-does-not-exist and it can't live without her.

Two sound holes hanging suspended in the air between a turban and some drapery are all that remains of Man Ray's 1924 photograph *Le violon d'Ingres* after Grove's retouching of it. The violin was never a violin in the first place but the back of the legendary Kiki — model to Utrillo, Soutine, and Foujita, and both model and mistress to Man Ray. Man Ray's biographer, Janus, described her as a "woman in love," "happy in her nudity," a "rare companion who understood the needs of an artist, . . . a part of France that was destined to disappear." And disappear she dutifully did, from both Man Ray's life and the history of art. Kiki returned to being Alice Prin, a working-class girl from Brittany, and her photograph reappeared only as part of the collection of the bourgeois and now respectable Mr. and Mrs. Man Ray.

However, the photograph immediately became famous and gained considerable market value. An homage to Ingres, it combined the back of the painter's famous Turkish bather with a reference to his favorite hobby, violin playing, while itself playing upon the French expression for a hobby, *un violon d'Ingres*. Played upon Kiki's back, the work resounds upon the rakish old tune about playing one's mistress like a musical instrument. In 1971 both the Ingres and the Man Ray were exhibited together in the Louvre, and "thus," explains Janus, "Man Ray's work, too, has become a classic." How "thus"? On Kiki's back, apparently. But a classic is not made off the back of one woman alone — to create a classic tradition you need

many, many nude women. Man Ray, in quoting Ingres, was enlisting the service of all those broad backs of Ingres's bathers who sit on soft cushions and gaze vacuously upon mounds and mounds of female flesh at their toilette. Like Man Ray, Grove mines earlier works of art, but because she is undermining the assumptions upon which the tradition is founded, her photograph will not "thus" become a classic. Nor is Grove's quotation an homage to the "original"; it is not even a quotation in the standard sense, but places the "classic" in quotation marks.

Kathy Grove was born in 1948 in Pittsburgh. She received a B.F.A. from the Rhode Island School of Design and an M.F.A. from the University of Wisconsin at Madison. Parts of "The Other Series" have been the subject of solo exhibits at Pace/MacGill Gallery, P.P.O.W. Gallery, and the University Art Museum of California State University at Long Beach. She now lives in New York City.

The Other Series: After Man Ray   1990

The Guerrilla Girls, an anonymous group of women who call themselves the conscience of the art world, do battle against sexism and racism in the art world with "facts, humor, and fake fur." Armed with statistics about the exclusionary exhibition and editorial practices of museums, galleries, art magazines, critics, and curators, these masked avengers began their war against discrimination by plastering the streets of SoHo with posters during the nights of 1985. The information they made public left no doubt that in the midst of the boom of the eighties, the art world was backsliding. The Guerrilla Girls pointed a critical finger at double standards, they named names, they shocked and embarrassed an art world that was revealed to be far more racist and sexist than even the general population. They made many people uncomfortable and defensive, others laugh, and everyone aware. Soon they were invited into more mainstream venues — Artforum, Mirabella, Ms., Vogue, and even The New York Times ran features on them. In 1987 they organized an alternative to the Whitney Museum of American Art Biennal exhibition, documenting the steadily declining numbers of women and artists of color exhibited by a museum that purported to be the museum of American art. In less than a

Guerrilla Girls

decade they have gained international recognition, been invited to speak in numerous locations, and made various television and radio appearances in the United States, Europe, Canada, South America, and Australia. Recently, they became the subject of an award-winning documentary film, Guerrillas in Our Midst, and this year saw the publication of their book Confessions of the Guerrilla Girls.

The Guerrilla Girls have managed to move the feminist critique from biological determinism to a consideration of gender positions systemic within a particular power structure. Their work, like all feminist activity, is a calculatedly optimistic gesture and thus may be accused of utopianism, or at least participation in what Steven Connor has referred to as "the romance of the margins," that is, a belief in the subversive potential of the marginal condition. But women are the least likely to regard their marginal condition as "romance." The romantic notion of the "outsider" artist working alone in his [sic] studio has continued to be a convenient myth for male artists, who from time to time may affect the role, but for women artists working in isolation this myth is bleak reality. The Guerrilla Girls have rewritten this particular romance in a poster called "The Advantages of Being a Woman Artist." Some of these advantages include "Working without the pressure of success. Not having to be in shows with men. Having an escape from the art world in your 4 free-lance jobs. Being reassured that whatever kind of art you make it will be labeled feminine. Not having to undergo the embarrassment of being called a genius. Not being stuck in a tenured teaching position. Knowing your career might pick up after you are eighty."

If women artists have been working at the margins, it is because that has been the only site available to them. But by using the subversive strategy of laughter, the Guerrilla Girls turned the culturally marginal position to which they had always been relegated into the new frontier. Rather than a condition of disenfranchisement, they have used the margin as a strategic site of deployment, an agency of intervention — pluralizing, destabilizing, baffling the centered and hierarchical discourse in which they, as artists and as women, inevitably find themselves.

The Guerrilla Girls can be contacted at 532 LaGuardia Place #237, New York, NY 10012.

THE ADVANTAGES OF BEING A WOMAN ARTIST:

- Working without the pressures of success.
- Not having to be in shows with men.
- Having an escape from the art world in your 4 free-lance jobs.
- Knowing your career might pick up after you are eighty.
- Being reassured that whatever kind of art you make it will be labeled feminine.
- Not being stuck in a tenured teaching position.
- Seeing your ideas live on in the work of others.
- Having the opportunity to choose between career and motherhood.
- Not having to choke on those big cigars or paint in Italian suits.
- Having more time to work after your mate dumps you for someone younger.
- Being included in revised versions of art history.
- Not having to undergo the embarrassment of being called a genius.
- Getting your picture in art magazines wearing a gorilla suit.

A PUBLIC SERVICE MESSAGE FROM **GUERRILLA GIRLS** CONSCIENCE OF THE ARTWORLD
532 LaGUARDIA PLACE, #237 • NY, NY 10012

Do women have to be naked to get into the Met. Museum?

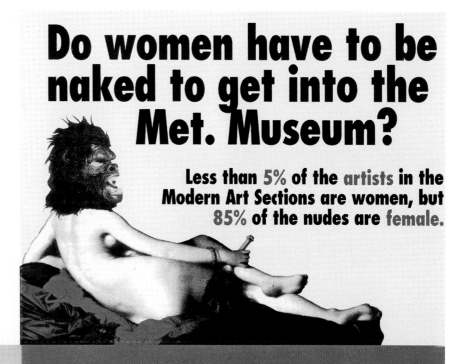

Less than 5% of the artists in the Modern Art Sections are women, but 85% of the nudes are female.

BUS COMPANIES ARE MORE ENLIGHTENED THAN NYC ART GALLERIES.

% women in the following jobs:

Bus Drivers	49.2%
Sales Persons	48%
Managers	43%
Mail Carriers	17.2%
Artists represented by 33 major NYC art galleries	16%
Truck Drivers	8.9%
Welders	4.8%

A PUBLIC SERVICE MESSAGE FROM **GUERRILLA GIRLS** CONSCIENCE OF THE ARTWORLD
532 LaGUARDIA PLACE, #237 • NY, NY 10012

GUERRILLA GIRLS' POP QUIZ.

Q. if February is Black History Month and March is Women's History Month, what happens the rest of the year?

A. Discrimination.

A PUBLIC SERVICE MESSAGE FROM **GUERRILLA GIRLS** CONSCIENCE OF THE ARTWORLD
532 LaGUARDIA PLACE, #237 • NY, NY 10012

To write a quality cliché you have to come up with something new.
— Jenny Holzer

Jenny Holzer

Jenny Holzer first entered the streets surreptitiously, putting up posters that were quickly covered over in the general pell-mell of street advertising. Holzer speaks of the streets as both the site of her artistic origins and an arena she feels the need to return to: "It's necessary for me to continue to practice outside. This is where my work went originally, and where I still feel it operates best." Over the past ten years her work has become "street clothes" appearing on building walls, billboards, movie marquees, wall plaques, light-emitting diodes (LEDs), shopping bags, matchbooks, T-shirts, and baseball caps. On the dilapidated movie marquees of the now-condemned buildings of New York's red-light district on 42nd Street one of Holzer's signs asks, "What urge will save you now that sex won't?"

Holzer is engaged in a process of compounding cliché upon cliché, as if to beat the stultifying force of language at its own game. As Fredric Jameson points out, the symbolic order is the source of meaning and, at the same time, "the source of all cliché, the very fountainhead of all those more debased 'meaning-effects' which saturate our culture." Holzer plays upon the codes already in place, the reality that has already been written for us, to make us aware of the ways in which those clichés have saturated us — the degree to which we are shaped by the verbal environment in which we are immersed.

Truisms (1978-79) and *Inflammatory Essays* (1977-82) arrest the repeater of language in the act of conformity, in the conditioned acceptance of some platitude, some authoritative statement, some adage by which one habitually conducts one's life. Like Flaubert's *Dictionary of Accepted Ideas*, Holzer's *Truisms* replace thought with formulaic statements: "Don't place too much trust in experts," "Don't run people's lives for them," "Everyone's work is equally important," "You must remember you have freedom of choice," "Children are the hope of the future." It is due to the sheer multiplicity of these truths and the rapidity with which the viewer is presented with the next, equally valid but often contradictory truth ("Exceptional people deserve special concessions," "People are nuts if they think they control their lives," "Children are the cruelest of all") that the displacement occurs. The *Inflammatory Essays* have the didactic tone of the *Book of Ecclesiastes*, with its transcendent source of information, and they have the typeface of the *New York Times* headlines, another signifier of Truth, but the authority of the text is undermined by the sheer multiplicity of conflicting truths moving the reader in and out of the realm of the absurd.

Holzer observes that women artists are more likely to deal with what she called "real world subject matter" because women "do sense real danger from forces like institutions, for example. Hence we address them in our work." Language is clearly the institution Holzer has felt most endangered by. Her aim seems to be to push language past the point where it could exert any control over her, past sense into the realm of the sensual. To enter a Holzer installation is to enter what Bakhtin calls a *grammatica jocosa*, a thoroughly material metaphysics in which the grotesque is bodied forth in the language itself. What is emitted by Holzer's light-emitting diodes is the erotic, the obscene, the materially satisfying non-sense. The broken, repeated sentences that wash over the spectator are fragments torn from the structural dyads of carnival: high and low, birth and agony, food and excrement, curses and praises, laughter and tears.

Jenny Holzer was born in 1950 in Gallipolis, Ohio. She received a B.F.A. from Ohio University and an M.F.A. from the Rhode Island School of Design. She was the American representative in the 44th Venice Biennale in 1990, at which she received the Leone d'Oro. She now lives in New York City.

If the mother who knows sexual pleasure, the subject of Mary Kelly's earlier work *Post-Partum Document*, is the most severely repressed "feminine" figure in Western culture, then the middle-aged woman runs a close second. If the assumption of an image occasions desire, then middle age marks the loss of that assumed image, of not being the object of man's desire, of being out of sync with how one looks, of alienation from one's image. It is this arbitrary application of significance to image that links *Interim* to the hysterical inscriptions invented by Charcot. What the work discloses is that the image of the woman, the hysteric, is not a pedagogic prop but a contested terrain.

Interim (1983-85) explores representations of aging, specifically the way women are represented. Kelly selects ordinary objects, particularly items of women's clothing, and, following the mechanism of the fetish, substitutes the object for the lack: shoes, the classic fetish object, or lacy slip. Underclothing, Freud noted, are often chosen as a fetish. They

Mary Kelly

"crystallize the moment of undressing, the last moment in which the woman could still be regarded as phallic." The clothes are folded, opened or knotted, and captioned according to Charcot's classifications of the photographs or drawings of women's bodies in the "passionate attitudes" of hysteria in his *Iconographie photographique de la Salpêtrière:* "Menacé," "Appel," "Supplication," "Erotisme," "Extase." For each attitude there are three positions, each captioned in a different typeface to suggest the way sexuality is inscribed in a number of discourses, such as fashion and beauty, popular medicine, sexology, or romantic fiction. The images (laminated positives on perspex) attain a "presence," that is, they cast a shadow on a fleshy pink background suggestive of makeup. They act as a mirror in which the viewer catches her own reflection. This drama reenacts Lacan's mirror stage which he saw as:

> a drama whose internal thrust is precipitated from insufficiency to anticipation — and which manufactures for the subject, caught up in the lure of spatial identification, the succession of phantasies that extends from a fragmented body-image to a form of its totality that I shall call orthopaedic — and, lastly, to the assumption of the armor of an alienating identity, which will rank with its rigid structure the subject's entire mental development.

In *Interim* Kelly effects a displacement; the identification with the woman observed is transferred to the article of clothing — a metonymy, not a presence. In Kelly's narrative we are told that the black leather jacket is the orthopaedic prop, the armor, worn by the woman attempting to signify "professional artist." Each image is accompanied by a text, a compilation of conversations with women — women who are *listened to* rather than *looked at* — as in "the talking cure."

Mary Kelly was born in Iowa in 1941. She studied in Florence at Pius XII Institute and in London at St. Martin's School of Art. A selection of her writings is forthcoming from MIT Press. Her most recent installation *Gloria Patria* is currently travelling in Europe. She now lives in New York City.

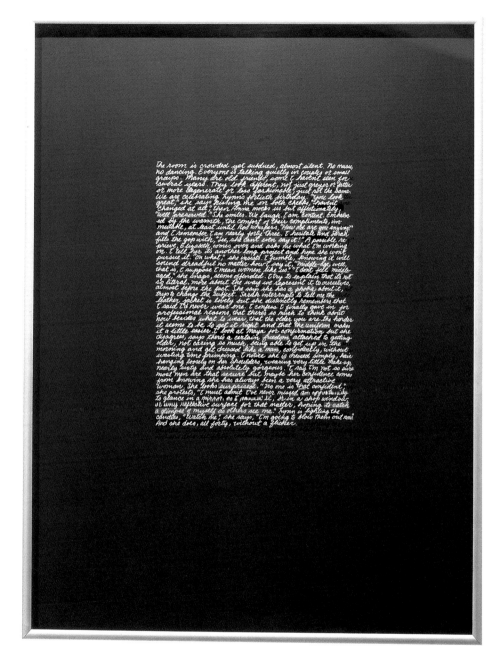

MENACÉ

Menacé, from *Interim Part 1: Corpus*   1984-85

I want to be on the side of pleasure and laughter and to disrupt the dour certainties of pictures, property, and power.
—Barbara Kruger

Barbara Kruger puts her art out to play in the constant traffic of consumer messages — on posters, signs, matchboxes, postcards, placards, billboards, museum walls, even on the bodies of passersby in the form of T-shirts or shopping bags. Although the early work may have been more psychoanalytically inflected and the later work more focused on late capitalism's consumerism, it always addresses the complex interconnection of

he's telling another one — about broads. And I thought, Oh, that's me. So the jokes are never addressed *to* me, they're *about* me. I can't laugh about that. Because this is a triangulation in which we, as women, are spoken of but never addressed. We are never a subject, we are always an object."

Kruger didn't need to read Freud to understand the mechanism of the smutty joke — she just needed to be female. The woman, who is taken as object of the hostile or sexual aggressiveness, is a necessary conduit for this form of exchange between men. The joke functions as a bond between teller and listener. The listener responds to the joke by laughing and is

Barbara Kruger

gender and the marketplace. As women, she says, "we loiter outside trade and speech and are obliged to steal language." Although she, perhaps more than most artists working today, is aware of the various and complex ways women are victimized in mass culture, she does not suffer from agoraphobia. "I wanted my work to enter the marketplace," Kruger explains, "because I began to understand that outside the market there is nothing." And her phrases are the colloquialisms of that marketplace, printed on severely cropped commercial photographs in Helvetica Bold, the signature typeface of postindustrial capitalism: **Buy me I'll change your life . . . when I hear the word culture I take out my checkbook . . . money can buy you love . . . I shop therefore I am . . . put your money where your mouth is.**

As a teller of tendentious jokes, Kruger is acutely aware of their gender dynamics: "I remember watching Johnny Carson one night 15 years ago. He was telling a joke and I was laughing along with Johnny. He finishes that joke and suddenly

thereby won over into a pseudo-identification with the teller by "the effortless satisfaction of his own libido." Kruger disrupts this male bonding by telling obscene jokes of her own. By "obscene" I mean overexposed, overly revealing; she is telling them "in mixed company," addressing an audience that includes the women who are supposed to be absent. Kruger refers to her project as a "series of attempts to welcome the female spectator into the audience of men."

Freud's analysis of the mechanism of the dirty joke that traps the listener into a pseudo-identication with the teller is much the same as Lacan's concept of the spectator's relation to representation, in which both listener and spectator are fixed in their place, "arrested" by "the dialectic of identificatory haste." **Your gaze hits the side of my face**, written down the side of a photograph of a marble bust of a woman, speaks of the stultifying effect of the sadistic gaze. Immobility, particularly the immobility of women, is a recurrent theme in Kruger's work, as in **We have received orders not to move** printed across the image of a seated woman, who is hunched forward and held in place with pins. **You are a captive audience**, the viewer is told, but this fixity, this stereotype is exactly what Kruger is undoing. Here at last we can understand what jokes achieve. "Jokes produce freedom," Freud notes, "undoing the renunciation and retrieving what was lost. . . . We can only laugh when a joke has come to our help." Although Kruger's famous accusatory "You" seems specifically addressed to the male viewer, the help her jokes offer is not gender-exclusive. The "We" her work addresses is any subject seeking to shift the limits of his or her enclosure — through laughter.

Barbara Kruger was born in Newark, New Jersey, in 1945. She was educated at Syracuse University and Parsons School of Design. Recently she has been working on a number of outdoor public projects in the United States and Germany. She now lives in New York and Los Angeles.

Untitled (Memory Is Your Image of Perfection) 1982

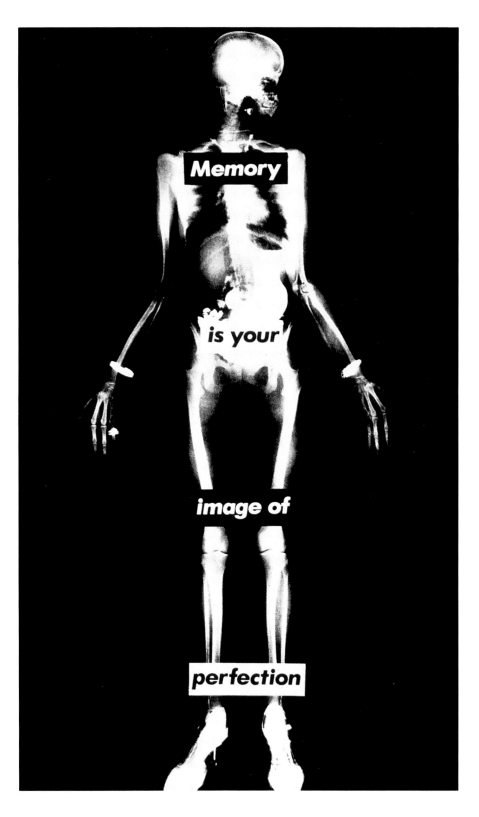

Irina Nakhova

Irina Nakhova explores the construction of gender as if it were the by-product of all cultural production. For several years Nakhova has been examining the interstices between process and completion, between fragmentation and wholeness, between the extant and the ruined, between renewal and decay. This began with a series of paintings called *Scaffoldings*, in which the image was of the scaffolding itself, the structures of restoration, not on what was being restored — a natural response to living in a culture caught up in *perestroika*.

After visiting Italy in 1987 she began another series exploring the ruins and remnants of classical antiquity; in the process she seems to have discovered, almost as if by accident, the gender assumptions upon which classical art is based. The perfect beauty of classical sculpture, with all its images of the finished, completed man, outwardly monolithic, is re-presented by Nakhova as inwardly riven. She subjects the classical body to the process of aging and decay, treating it like the material body. On wooden boards she has painted pairs of male and female faces or torsos that resemble antique relief sculpture. As classical statuary they show the usual effects of time in the form of chips and broken limbs, but Nakhova also gives them sags and wrinkles. All the pairs are cracked; in one set the cracks appear in a random pattern suggesting age or accident, while in another they appear along the lines of a perfectly symmetrical grid. The cracks are identical so that the viewer can exchange the pieces as in a jigsaw puzzle, and in doing so, the dichotomies between the material body, with its close association to the maternal body, and the classical body, with its claims to completion and perfection, become as apparent as the differences between the male and female bodies to which these dichotomies are inextricably associated.

In another interactive installation, entitled *Friends and Neighbors* (1994), Nakhova continues the exploration of the classical body in a contemporary context. She paints life-size torsos of ancient Greek statuary on old overcoats collected from secondhand shops in Moscow. The viewer is again invited to interact with the work. This is ready-to-wear art; one can try on the ideal body, try on a different sex if desired. In a version of this installation, with electrical engineering by Per Biorn, the coats are displayed on dressmaker's dummies; when touched, these headless perfect bodies respond by talking back to the viewer. Vituperative, seductive, nonsensical, or foreign speech, voicing the desires and anxieties of the contemporary self, emanate from these coolly classical bodies painted on shabby old overcoats.

Irina Nakhova was born in Moscow in 1955 and studied at the Moscow Institute of Graphic Arts. Recent solo exhibitions of her work have been held at Phyllis Kind Gallery in New York, Gallery 60 in Umea, Sweden, and the Cranbrook Art Museum. Currently she divides her time among Detroit, New York City, and Moscow.

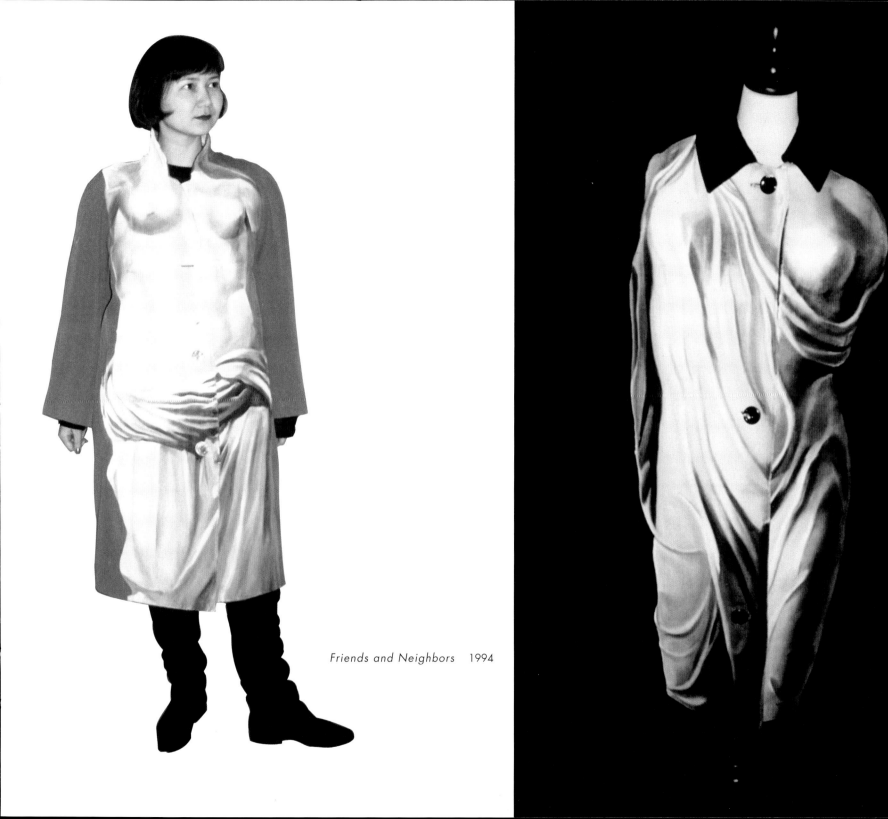

Friends and Neighbors 1994

Lorraine O'Grady

Every theory of subjectivity is a question of the body.
— Merleau-Ponty

Lorraine O'Grady's work is a mapping, or rather a re-mapping, of the black female body. She is a postcolonial cartographer on a journey of reclamation: the reclamation of the black female body as a site of subjectivity. What her work as a performance artist over the years reveals is just how the questions asked of the body determine the answers given. In the beginning, the body in question was her own. She made her debut in 1981 dressed in the masquerade of the beauty queen: floor-length white gown, rhinestone-and-pearl tiara, long white gloves, and beauty-pageant sash proclaiming her "Mademoiselle Bourgeoise Noire 1955." As she moved through the crowd, smiling and passing out flowers from her bouquet, a cat-o'-nine-tails was revealed entwined at its core. She became, then, in punning reversal, a "bête noir" — a frenzied, self-lacerating Dominatrix.

"Performance is the way I write most effectively," O'Grady has said, and we are not likely to get a clearer articulation of what it feels like to be a black woman forced into patriarchy's mould of white female pulchritude, except perhaps from O'Grady herself, who has argued in "Olympia's Maid: Reclaiming Black Female Subjectivity" that within the West's construction of the female body, the "femininity" of the white female body is ensured by assigning the nonwhite female body a place "outside what can be conceived of as woman."

Searching for a positive image of the self, O'Grady found her likeness reflected back to her in Egypt's contemporary heterogeneous cultural and racial amalgam as well as in its ancient monuments. On a visit to Cairo she was constantly mistaken for an Egyptian, but since all identity is based upon a misrecognition, O'Grady turned this "mistake" into the basis of an ongoing meta-narrative on racial/cultural encounter,

dispersion, and hybridization. Egypt, particularly because of what it represents to African Americans, provided a fertile terrain for O'Grady's project of reclamation.

In an ongoing series involving both photography and performance, O'Grady maps out the correspondences between the women of her own family and the women in Egyptian Queen Nefertiti's dynastic line. *Nerfertiti/Devonia Evangeline*, first performed in 1980, uses her own family to trace the African American diaspora through both contemporary American culture and ancient Egyptian art and mythology. From this performance evolved the *Miscegenated Family Album* series of 1980-88. In this work are formed sisterhoods linking, not just generations, but centuries of mixed-race women. O'Grady juxtaposes images of her sister, Devonia Evangeline, with images of Queen Nerfertiti; images of herself with ones of Nefertiti's younger sister, Mutnedjmet; and images of Devonia Evangeline's two daughters with images of Nefertiti's two daughters, creating a sense of an ancient and ongoing sisterhood based upon uncanny physical resemblance as well as similarities in family history.

O'Grady is fully aware that the quest for "origin" and "identity" is problematic from a poststructuralist point of view; nevertheless, for displaced persons the development of an effective relationship to place or to a lost ancestry becomes a means of recuperating a personal and cultural identity. O'Grady is not so much concerned with writing a story of origin as she is with writing over the narratives and images of a colonial culture that all but obliterated a previously extant culture. Her own idiosyncratic quest for subjectivity is used to politicize an aesthetics of identity.

Lorraine O'Grady received a B.A. from Wellesley College and an M.F.A. from the University of Iowa. She is a recipient of the Mary Ingraham Bunting Fellowship at Radcliffe College for 1995-96. Her *Miscegenated Family Album* will be on exhibit in 1996 at the Louisiana Museum of Modern Art in Copenhagen. She lives and works in New York City.

Sisters IV from *Miscegenated Family Album*   1980-88

Corporeal mapping is the subject of Kathy Prendergast's *Body Map* series, eleven exquisitely detailed ink and watercolor drawings done in 1983. Maps are talismanic in that they give us our bearings in the physical world, align us with something beyond and greater than ourselves and, at the same time, flatter us by giving us a sense of control over the area mapped. Prendergast's body maps disturb our belief in correspondences and reveal the very sinister underpinnings of this faith. These maps reveal the psychological interconnectedness between the activities of exploration and mapmaking, the desire to scrutinize, inscribe, and control the female body, and the colonial control of other lands through mapping and naming.

Kathy Prendergast

These are intricately drawn maps of what appears to be a large continental land mass surrounded by a pale blue sea. Numerous codes of cartography attest to the veracity of the map: the precision of the drawing, the heavy antique vellum paper, a compass rose indicating the four directions, sailing ship insignia indicating the separation of the seas from the land mass, and, of course, the division into a grid indicating longitude and latitude. These cartographic conventions are reassuring in their familiar logic and confident scientism; however, the land mass being mapped is not a continent but a female torso. The body is represented as a map, a manifestation of the Nietzschean notion of the body as a surface of social inscriptions, revealing what is at stake for women in the notion of the body as a surface of libidinal and erotogenic intensities inscribed and reinscribed by social norms, practices, and values.

The seeming rationalism and objectivity of mapmaking belie an underlying irrationality. The body maps are neither as obvious nor as stable as they first appear, and they can lead the explorer into dangerous terrain. The torso in the first drawing is life-size, and while it is unclear who is traversing this continent, or what the purpose of the journey is, the traveller must be microscopically tiny, smaller even than the Lilliputians in the land of Brobdingnag. The map is divided into quadrants, and subsequent maps are enlargements of these four sections. Now the scale is four times life-size, causing the activity depicted on the maps to become correspondingly smaller. These maps, too, can be subdivided and enlarged for closer scrutiny, on into infinity. Ptolemy's conceptual organization of the surface of the earth into a rectilinear grid may be reassuring to some, but in Prendergast's works it is the grid formation itself that is frightening. The grid enables, *generates* this progressive decompartmentalization that results in an expansion of each section of the body. When examined through a magnifying glass, the charts reveal yet more detail, suggesting that the exploration could lead to an infinite regression. Meanwhile, at the other end of the scale, the female body grows ever larger, more unfathomable, gargantuan. Like Gulliver, we can imagine falling into the crater of a hair follicle or being drowned by the volcanic emissions of a breast.

Gradually the viewer comes to realize that the source of the anxiety is not the female body but rather the terrifying relentlessness of the rational examination itself. The pathology thought to inhere in the female body resides instead in the desire to control it, the proliferation of methods of exploitation, the obsessional need for more and more detailed information, the constant quest for correspondence to an ideal.

Kathy Prendergast was born in Dublin, Ireland, in 1958. She received a B.A. from the National College of Art and Design in Dublin and an M.F.A. from the Royal College of Art in London. She was awarded the Premio Duemila award for best young artist at the 1995 Venice Biennale. She now lives and works in London.

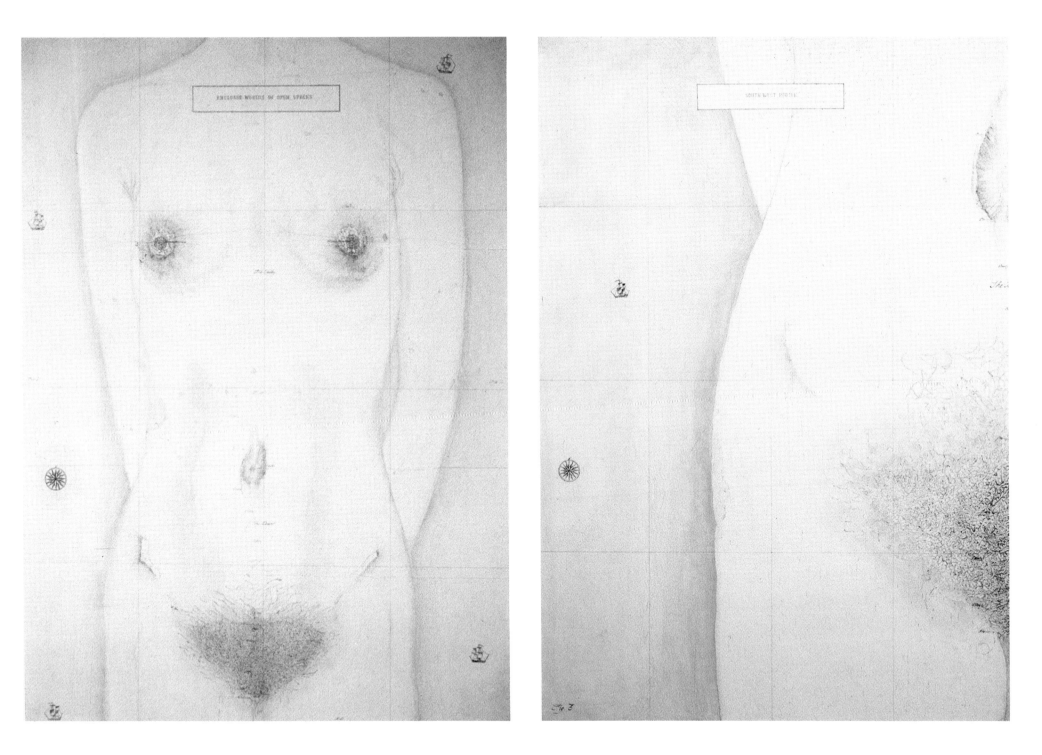

In a bus shelter in Vancouver I saw a poster proclaiming, "*We* are the first world, *You* are the third." The poster points with economy and humor to the power of subject positions in our speech, to how dichotomies of "we" and "they" are established, and how commonplace understandings about others form *our* identity. Like Tonto, when the frantic Lone Ranger cries,"Tonto, the Indians have us surrounded — we're done for!" Elaine Reichek asks, "Who's *we*, white man?" Good question. What is the subject position of the second sex in the first world? Is it the same as that of the first sex in the third world? It's hard to compute, and *we* women are notoriously bad at math.

Reichek's installations begin with information, material culled from the vast storehouses of photographs, documents, and artifacts accumulated during the heyday of the encyclopedic urge that so preoccupied the first world at the close of the last

Elaine Reichek

century. The burgeoning museum culture ostensibly grew out of the desire to preserve a record of peoples and customs before they vanished. But what was really about to vanish was the era of colonial expansionism: these are fragments we have shored against *our* ruin.

Reichek addresses museum practices, but the project is not about the failure of the museum to produce "truth" or an objective account of other peoples. Nor is it about first-world culpability. Rather, she is accumulating texts about textuality, about fabrication, and about the ways in which we are fashioned by our own fabrications. Reichek reads our documentation of other peoples for their symptomatology, for what they tell us of our needs and desires. She is not the Ralph Nader of a museum culture, demanding correct consumer

information. She is an eccentric and generous reader who finds herself constitutionally alienated from divisions like "fact" and "fiction" and doesn't hold text or teller accountable for the misinformation they generate. Instead, "errors" become cracks that provide an opportunity to look behind the texts to the culture that requires them.

There is a flagrant and funny feminism weaving in and around Reichek's reworking of ethnographic, anthropological, and museum exhibition practices. It is most overtly manifested in her choice of the medium of knitting, which she uses to reproduce documentary photographs of native peoples and their dwellings. Knitting is an "inappropriate" tool for this purpose — so unscientific, one of those typically feminine misunderstandings. It is as if she had taken literally Barthes's metaphor of the textuality of the text: "Text means *tissue*, but whereas hitherto we have always taken this tissue as a product, a ready-made veil, behind which lies, more or less hidden, meaning (truth), we are now emphasizing, in the tissue, the generative idea that the text is made, is worked out in a perpetual interweaving; lost in this tissue — this texture — the subject unmakes himself, like a spider dissolving in the constructive secretions of its web."

It is our erotic body that Reichek invites us to explore. The knitted bodies offer the pleasures of texture and proximity. They have a plenitude, a warmth, a sensuality. Their tactility implicitly invites us to touch or rub these nude or seminude fuzzy bodies, ambiguous fusions of cuddly lifesize doll and dark, enigmatic, even slightly threatening Other.

Elaine Reichek was born in New York. She received a B.F.A. from Yale University and a B.A. from Brooklyn College. Recent solo exhibitions have been held at the Irish Museum of Modern Art (1993), Stichting de Appel, Amsterdam (1994), The Jewish Museum, New York (1995), and the Wexner Center for the Arts, Columbus, Ohio (1995). She lives in New York City.

Nietzsche's complaint that woman is always acting, that every woman is an artist, is the underlying premise of Cindy Sherman's work. Sherman is the model for her images: her early works are self-portraits that ironically reveal the categorical contradiction of the genre. She is Everywoman, and womanliness itself is a masquerade. If this reminds you of Epimenides's paradox of self-reference along the lines of "All women are liars . . . I am a woman," it shows how far Sherman takes us into the defiles of the signifier. In the late 1970s she

began taking black-and-white photos reminiscent of the *femme fatales* of *film noir*. In these elaborations of images of women caught in the middle of ambiguous narratives, she is a woman demonstrating the representations of woman, and the pose is presented *as* pose.

The masquerade of "femininity" may function either as a form of complicity with, or refusal of, patriarchal sexual relations. Sandra Lee Bartky notes that "the woman who checks her makeup half a dozen times a day to see if her foundation has caked or her mascara has run . . . has become, just as surely as the inmate of the Panopticon, a self-policing subject, self-committed to a relentless self-surveillance. This self-surveillance is a form of obedience to patriarchy." In a classic Lacanian double-bind, masquerade is the very definition of "femininity" because it is constructed entirely with reference to the male sign. Adopting it as a strategy is a risky gesture. Like the swimmer in Stevie Smith's poem "Not Waving, But Drowning," the masquerader can't be sure they won't think she is just waving, when really she's drowning.

When the mask begins to slip — when the construction of identity shows, as it does progressively in Sherman's work — the threat behind the mask of womanliness is revealed. Images of

Sherman in *Vogue* magazine modelling clothing by the designer Dorothée Bis were part of a proliferation of images of hysterics in high fashion, but Sherman pushes the grotesque too far, turning the fashionable into the pathological, presenting them as part of the same continuum. In more recent work the body is either replaced by prosthetic devices or by body fragments: the parts we have always mistaken for the whole, as Lacan points out in his theory of the imaginary. The body fragments Sherman presents are the bizarre yet familiar fragments that cinema

Cindy Sherman

presents; the body in cinema is either fragmented by the viewing apparatus, or the body itself is chopped up, sawn, rent, or scattered across the visual field. Appropriately, it is in his study entitled *Television* that Lacan calls upon us to witness the hysteric:

> Man does not think with his soul, as the Philosopher
> imagined. He thinks as a consequence of the fact that
> a structure, that of language — the word implies it — a
> structure carves up his body, a structure that has nothing to
> do with anatomy. Witness the hysteric. This shearing
> happens to the soul through the obsessional symptom:
> a thought that burdens the soul, that it doesn't know
> what to do with.

Sherman is the witness for the hysteric. In her early work, language carves up her body the way paper dolls are cut out; she constructs herself through the identities fashioned by the prevailing representational modes of Hollywood films and fashion magazines. At first the split in the subject could be thought of as the split between the subject of the gaze, the socially constructed subject, and the "real" subject it presumably

conceals. Hence the fascination with what the "real" Cindy Sherman looks like, but the "real" Cindy Sherman has disappeared into her own appearance. Through her long obsession with an identity's undoing she has discovered, not the dispossessed body in the imaginary, but the possessed body of the hysteric: a body that ages, splits, vomits, bleeds, and symptomatizes, a body subject to paralyses and anaesthesias. In refusing an identity by proffering multiples, in fragmenting and dispersing the body, in becoming the grotesque, in adopting the hysteric's gesture of resistance, Sherman does not cede her desire.

Cindy Sherman was born in 1954 in Glen Ridge, New Jersey. She received a B.A. from the State University of New York at Buffalo. In 1995 she was awarded a MacArthur Foundation Grant. She lives and works in New York City

Untitled   1984

Language weighs heavily upon the body in Jeanne Silverthorne's work, perhaps because she gives it weight, embodies it in sculptural form, or perhaps because in her work language always represents loss or damage to the body. The sculptures are extensions of the body, a body in the process of speaking. The early sculptures — the *Gossip* series (1982-84) — were modelled on prosthetic devices and linked to small monosyllabic words: attached to a knee-brace is the word "Too," perhaps to say "too bad"; a pair of dentures clatter the criticism, "So, So"; a leg support says, "Says," as if implying that it is in on the cutting circuit of gossip of who says what about whom. The pairing suggests that language is a kind of prosthesis enabling the user to extend her influence beyond the physical limitations of the body, but at the same time there is a sense of impairment, a recognition of the damage done to the body by language. Language can be used as a crutch, but a kind of symbiosis sets in: the body is disfigured by its dependency. In other works, inanimate objects are anthropomorphized and seem to be on the verge of speech: a hydrocal faucet issues what looks like a steady stream of water down a drain that says "Sorry"; a tongue oozing from a hot-water bottle gurgles

of apotheosis of the dysfunctional.

Running throughout Silverthorne's sculptural work is a play upon another language, that of art history. Her flaccid rubber versions of commonplace objects are rife with references to Oldenburg; the light bulbs are a direct quotation from Jasper Johns; the clouds are like Bernini's cumulus cushions; while the sexuality implicit in these anthropomorphic inanimate objects speaks to the work of Eva Hesse and Louise Bourgeois. *Correspondences*, an ongoing series of small sculptures, letters, and photographs, is an attempt to address directly the activity of producing and reproducing a work of art. The smale-scale sculptures are themselves modelled upon much smaller fragments of plaster fallen off larger moulds or hardened drippings of excess rubber or discarded lumps of clay, all from other projects. Always something is left over, something remains in excess of the language intended to encode it. Soon correspondences begin to emerge. Inevitably, once the randomly formed fragments are inserted into an art context (i.e., put on pedestals, exhibited in a gallery), they start to look like other works of art. Many resemble the sculptures of Rodin. Ironically, some even suggest classical statuary.

Jeanne Silverthorne

"Please"; a mass of budding matter proclaims "UP, UP, UP." Books snore; light bulbs, always the signifier of bright ideas, are given thought bubbles in which they think of themselves as abstractions, as pure signifiers; a huge chandelier, a complex ganglion of rubber cords illuminating nothing, becomes a kind

Exploring expression outside language, what it is like to be speechless matter, was the impetus for a large-scale female fertility figure loosely based on the Venus of Willendorf. In this sculpture the female body is reduced to its essential components, a fantasy of the mother's body with reproductive organs swollen and dominant. This is woman trapped in biology, encased in grotesque heaps of flesh, with nothing on, nor on her mind. In fact, she has almost no head at all; it seems to have atrophied, like all the rest of her unused appendages. Without arms, legs, or language, she is without agency, but since she is placed on a pedestal (actually a rubber dolly with wheels), she could, if inclined, slip away.

When a number of Silverthorne sculptures are shown together, the installation looks like a setup for a series of Rube Goldberg or Fischli & Weiss comic calamities — one accidental occurrence leading inevitably to the next. The only thing required to set it off is for someone or something to slip up. And there on the floor is a black rubber banana peel, something skinned, of course, but also the deus ex machina that turns it all into a joke.

Jeanne Silverthorne was born in Philadelphia in 1950. She received a B.A. and an M.A. from Temple University. An exhibition of her work will open in February 1996 at the ICA in Philadephia. She now lives in New York City.

Untitled   1989

Writing in 1855 on the essence of laughter, Baudelaire described it as the collision of two contraries and linked it with the accident of the ancient Fall. Like the Original Joke, the Fall threatened the established order of things; it was a spanner, a monkey wrench in the works. Baudelaire does not mention Eve in this account, but we know the story. It seems that the mother of us all is the origin not just of chaos, but of the comic. The work of Nancy Spero is an extended examination of our origins, of the license and lawlessness of laughter and of women. Her entire opus writes large what Baudelaire and Rabelais only hinted at — that women have always been on the laughing side, that women have a stake in laughter's indissoluble and essential relation to freedom.

Spero uses the same images of women again and again in different contexts, where they play different roles and interact differently across huge extended spaces. In each context a new historic sense penetrates these ancient, mythological, or modern images and gives them new meanings, but their traditional contents are kept intact: copulation, pregnancy, birth, growth, old age, disintegration, dismemberment. Images of the material body are considered ugly, Mikhail Bakhtin suggests, precisely because they are in a constant state of change: "They are contrary to the classic images of the finished, completed man, cleansed, as it were, of all the scoriae of birth and development." The examples he gives are the figurines of senile pregnant hags in the famous Kerch terra cotta collection: "There is nothing completed, nothing calm and stable in the bodies of these old hags. They combine a senile, decaying and deformed

flesh with the flesh of new life, conceived but as yet unformed." Most important, he notes, the old hags are laughing.

These are the female figures that appear in Spero's work. Sheela-na-Gig, a Celtic goddess of fertility and destruction, smiles wryly at the viewer as she reaches behind her legs to display an enormous vagina. The same obscene and humorous gesture is used by the old hag Baubo, a personification of the *cunnus*, who, when she finds Demeter in deep mourning over the death of her daughter, lifts her skirts and exposes herself, causing Demeter to laugh. Like the Sybil of Panzoult in Rabelais's novel, she lifts her skirts and shows the parts through which everything passes (the underworld, the grave) and from which everything issues forth. In the work done for the present

Nancy Spero

exhibition, Spero has Sheela link arms with Wilma, an aboriginal fertility goddess, in a comic chorus line, revealing what the flounces of the tutu usually carefully conceal.

These images have the opposite effect of fetishized images of women; they are not engaged in a cover-up. What was powerful or taboo or frightening in ordinary life is turned into amusing or ludicrous monstrosities. "Let the priests tremble," Spero quotes Hélène Cixous in one of her scrolls, "we're going to show them our sexts! Too bad for them if they fall apart upon discovering that women aren't men, or that the mother doesn't have one." The fear of Medusa as the archetypal symbol of castration and the abyss is, Cixous observes, a convenient fear. But Medusa's laugh defeats these fears; she is not hideous: "You have only to look at the Medusa straight on to see her. And she is not deadly. She is beautiful and she is laughing."

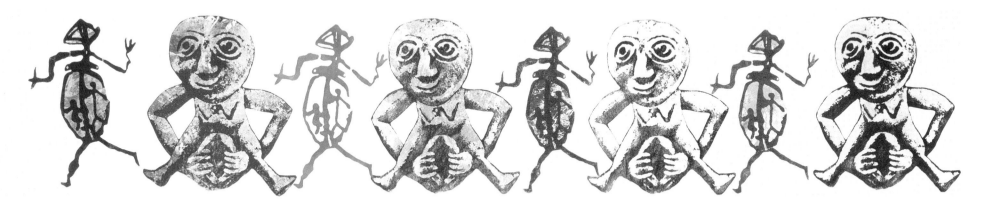

Sheela and Wilma   1985

The disruptive, ever-renewing laughter informing Spero's work is the antithesis of the static, hierarchical conception of the world required for the maintenance of a class and gender-based society. It travesties the established, the authorial, the didactic, the dogmatic. It is, above all, a challenge to ready-made solutions in the sphere of thought, to the accepted idea, to the established assumption and convention that construct the self-evident, what Wallace Stevens calls "the fatal, dominant X." Spero's work specifically targets what feminism has always targeted — things as they are, for things as they are are not for women.

Nancy Spero was born in Cleveland in 1926. After receiving a B.F.A. from the Art Institute of Chicago in 1949, she attended the École des Beaux-Arts and the Atelier André Lhote in Paris. She lives and works in New York City. A monograph on her work will appear in the Phaidon *Contemporary Artists* series in 1996.

Susan Unterberg

"Paternity may be a legal fiction," Joyce speculates in the episode of *Ulysses* in which the proprietary assumptions of man, both in the act of begetting and in the act of authorship, are brought into question. "Fatherhood, in the sense of consciousness begetting is unknown to man. It is founded upon the void, upon incertitude, upon unlikelihood. *Amor Matris*, subjective and objective genitive, may be the only true thing in life." Motherhood indeed may be the only fact of life about which we can be confident. The dyadic relationship in which the mother and child are undifferentiated beings, oblivious to the outside world and complete unto themselves can, however, only be experienced nostalgically. We can only know it, attempt to articulate it, when it is over. Thus the adult fantasy of a selfless love is always marked by a sense of loss. For all the biological certainty of birth, what mother, briefly desiring something beyond the child, has not wondered if this were really her child, and what child, unsatisfied with this site of origin, has not thought its real mother must be someone/somewhere else? "Whatever the individual mother's love and strength," Adrienne Rich writes in *Of Woman Born*, "the child in us, the small female who grew up in a male-controlled world, still feels, at moments, *wildly unmothered.*"

Susan Unterberg began her ongoing exploration of family relationships with a series of photographs of mothers and daughters in the *Mother Series* (1985). In addressing the construction of motherhood Unterberg is not dealing with a biological given but with a complex set of representations, suited to the needs of a particular social order, that circumscribes women's lives and imposes itself as reality. Historically the representation of motherhood has been in the hands of male artists or authors, and in Christianity and Freudian theory, the two main Western stories of the family (in which we all find ourselves inscribed, no matter what our personal beliefs), the mother is represented as the "conduit" from father to son. What does it mean to be a mother, asks Mary Jacobus, "when mothers are the waste product of a sexual system based on the exchange of women among men?"

Yet for various reasons women artists, searching for ways to represent women, have been slow to turn to what would seem an obvious source of reference — the image of their own mothers — perhaps because it is not an image they want for themselves or because this image of woman simply has not been presented, in art or anywhere else. Just to put forward these images of women and their mothers — ordinary women who are neither particularly young nor beautiful — is to disturb.

What strikes us first about Unterberg's photographs of mothers and daughters is their extraordinary honesty, an honesty that could come only with age, with difficulty, an honesty that perhaps could come only from a middle-aged woman. The images are straightforward, unaltered, unposed close-ups, the subjects instructed only not to smile and to look directly at the viewer. A series of seven photographs of each daughter is juxtaposed with seven photographs of her mother. The images are not constructed as narratives, yet they tell stories of pain, frustration, anger, ambivalence, even loneliness. Looking back and forth from mother to daughter, we see physical resemblances, the effects of aging, similarities in gestures and expressions, stories of what was and what will be, but also signs of the degree to which the daughter resist or accepts the mother's fate and of the mother's own rage or acquiescence.

The first portraits of the mother/daughter series are of Unterberg and her own mother. The artist speaks of identification with her mother, of the pain of her mother's illness and her unarticulated anger. At the same time Unterberg talks of "trying hard not to become my mother," not to accept the rules that governed the mother's life, the demands that the daughter be "pretty, pleasing, placating, to find a husband and have children." The aim of this installation is to reveal the cruelty masked by such trivialization. There is a kind of exhilaration in this unflattering presentation of self ("unlovable, an old woman,

Self-Portrait / Mother Series 1985

and bummed out"); worse yet, it is the presentation of all that we resist in our mothers, the self each of us will become in old age. Contrary to Sartre's claim that after forty we get the face we deserve, women after forty get the face they have the courage to present.

Susan Unterberg was born in New York City in 1941. She received a B.A. from Sarah Lawrence College in 1977 and an M.A. in Photography from New York University in 1985. Her most recent solo exhibition, *Close Ties*, was held at The New Museum of Contemporary Art in 1994. She lives in New York City.

Only jokes that have a purpose run the risk of meeting with people who do not want to listen to them. — Freud

In *Ain't Jokin'* (1987-88) Carrie Mae Weems tells a series of crude visual and verbal jokes based on racial stereotypes that aren't funny. Photographs of stereotypical blacks (a man with a watermelon or a woman with a leg of chicken) are combined with verbal "jokes" of the following sort: "What are the three things you can't give a black person? Answer: A black eye, a fat lip, and a job." In telling these jokes she is subverting the tendentious joke that depends for its effect upon the differences in the hearers' reactions. "Generally speaking, a tendentious joke calls for three people: in addition to the one who makes the joke, there must be a second who is taken as the object of the hostile or sexual aggressiveness, and a third in whom the joke's aim of producing pleasure is fulfilled" (Freud). By telling the joke herself, she removes herself from the role of object of the joke and is able to redirect the hostility. Also, in telling the joke herself, she is betraying a class secret: Freud points out that it is

the museum- and gallery-going white middle class, an audience whose social and educational level is assumed to be high and whose level of repression is also high. This audience may want to listen to them, but they want to pretend they've never heard them.

Still, telling white-trash jokes to a white bourgeois audience is nobody's idea of a good time, as *Mirror, Mirror* makes clear: "Looking into the mirror, the black woman asked, 'Mirror, mirror on the wall, who's the finest of them all?' The Mirror says, 'Snow White, you black bitch, and don't you forget it!'" Questions asked determine the answers given. Looking in the mirror held up by Anglo America is no way to develop a positive self-image, and so Weems went looking elsewhere. She travelled to the islands off the South Carolina–Georgia coast. Here she found in the landscape and household objects evidence of a rich and enduring black community. Its Gullah culture took root on a kind of Ellis Island for African Americans. Slave ships continued to land on these islands long after the slave trade had been banned; as many West Africans remained where they landed,

Carrie Mae Weems

only among what he calls the "inferior classes" that the tendentious or smutty joke is told in front of the person who is the object of the joke. At higher social levels ("civilization and higher education have a large influence in the development of repression") the joke is told only when the person who is the object of the hostility is not present. Weems tells these jokes to

African culture was maintained. But here one cannot trace one's ancestors through a computer search. Instead, as Weems shows us in *Sea Islands* (1992), some traces of them are more likely to be found reflected in the hubcaps and bicycle wheels hung in trees festooned with Spanish moss. What begins with grim daguerrotype photographs of slaves (originally mug shots, but here rephotographed, enlarged to life-size, framed in circular frames, and thus given the dignity of portraits) turns into a celebration of an enduring cultural heritage. Weems's own photographs depict mainly environments: neat rooms with simple furniture or storefronts advertising "Awesome Hair Performance" and "Sweet Potatoe Pies." The photographs are combined with red earthenware plates on which the artist has painted texts as poetic as the images, telling a tale of what was lost and what was found as she "Went Looking for Africa . . . and found it echoing in the voice of the Geechee's Gullah . . . Went Looking for Africa . . . and found a bowl of butter beans on a grave newspaper walls for the spirits to read rice in the corners a pan of vinegar water up under the bed . . . Went looking for Africa . . .and found uncombed heads acrylic nails & Afrocentric attitude Africans find laughable."

Carrie Mae Weems was born in 1953 in Portland, Oregon. She received a B.A. from the California Institute of the Arts and an M.F.A. from the University of California at San Diego. In 1994 she received the Louis Comfort Tiffany award. Her work will be on exhibit in the Project Room of the Museum of Modern Art in November 1995. She now lives in Brooklyn, N.Y.

Selections from Ain't Jokin'   1987-88

LOOKING INTO THE MIRROR, THE BLACK WOMAN ASKED, "MIRROR, MIRROR ON THE WALL, WHO'S THE FINEST OF THEM ALL?" THE MIRROR SAYS, "SNOW WHITE, YOU BLACK BITCH, AND DON'T YOU FORGET IT!!!"

List of Works

Dotty Attie

Mixed Metaphors 1993
oil on canvas
36 panels, each
15 x 15 cm
Courtesy P.P.O.W. Gallery

Origin of the World 1993
oil on linen
9 panels, each
15 x 15 cm
Courtesy P.P.O.W. Gallery

Marie Baronnet

Untitled 1994
color polaroids
2 series of 6,
each 20 x 21 cm

Dorothy Cross

Urinals 1992
cast bronze and hand-
painted signs
Britain: 74 x 43 x 48 cm
Ireland: 48 x 43 x 23 cm

Pap 1993
Guinness bottle & cow teat

Nancy Davidson

Overly Natural 1993
fabric, latex, wire

Nancy Dwyer

Big Ego 1990
polyurethane-coated nylon
3 letters, each approx.
244 x 142 x 223 cm

Ilona Granet

No Cat Calls 1987
enamel on metal
61 x 61 cm
Courtesy P.P.O.W. Gallery

Curb Your Animal Instincts 1986
enamel on metal
61 x 66 cm
Courtesy P.P.O.W. Gallery

Kathy Grove

*The Other Series:
After Lange* 1989-90
silver gelatin print
71 x 61 cm

*The Other Series:
After Man Ray* 1990
silver gelatin print
46 x 41 cm

*The Other Series:
After Matisse* 1989
c-print
61 x 53 cm

Guerrilla Girls

posters

Jenny Holzer

electric LED sign with red diodes
14 x 76 x 10 cm
Selections from *Truisms*
1986
Courtesy
Barbara Gladstone Gallery

Truisms 1977-82
offset ink on paper
each sheet
91 x 61 cm

Inflammatory Essays 1979-82
offset ink on paper
each sheet 26 x 26 cm

Mary Kelly

*Menacé, from Interim Part 1:
Corpus* 1984-85
laminated photo-positive
silkscreen and
acrylic on plexiglas
6 panels,
each 122 x 91 cm
Courtesy Postmasters

Barbara Kruger
Untitled (Memory Is Your
Image of Perfection) 1982
photograph
152 x 98 cm
Collection Henry S. McNeil, Jr.,
Philadelphia

The Revolutionary Power
of Women's Laughter 1982
Poster designed for
The Revolutionary Power
of Women's Laughter
exhibition January 15-
February 19, 1983.
Protetch McNeil, New York.

Irina Nakhova
with engineering by Per Biorn
Friends and Neighbors 1994
oil on coats
5 life-size mannequins
with coats

Lorraine O'Grady
Sisters IV from Miscegenated
Family Album 1980-88
cibachrome
4 diptychs,
each 27 x 38.5 cm
Courtesy Thomas Erben Gallery

Kathy Prendergast
Untitled, 1994
wool, filling, and motor
19 x 46 x 4 cms

Elaine Reichek
Yellow Man 1986
knitted wool and oil on photo
178 x 288 cm

Cindy Sherman
Untitled 1984
color photograph
128 x 190 cm
Courtesy Metro Pictures

Jeanne Silverthorne
Untitled 1989
hydrocal, rubber, and wheels
75 x 60 x 60 cm

Normal Skin IV 1989
rubber
43 x 56 x 7cm
Collection Susan Canning

Nancy Spero
Sheela and Wilma 1985
handprinting & printed
collage on paper
50 x 275 cm

Susan Unterberg
Self-Portrait / Mother Series
1985
color c-prints
315 x 35 cm

Carrie Mae Weems
Selections from *Ain't Jokin'*
1987-88
gelatin silver print and text
5 prints,
each 50 x 40 cm
Courtesy P.P.O.W. Gallery

In the beginning was the gest he joustly says, for the end is with woman, flesh without word.

James Joyce

Essay by Jo-Anna Isaak

"Reality is what has been written" (Roland Barthes) and we have only the poor freedom to accept or reject the text. With the acquisition of language comes only the ability to sign the pact others have written for us. We, in fact, do not "acquire" language—gaining access to the signifiers does not put us in any effective position in relation to them, rather the inverse is true—the speaking subject is subjected *to* and constructed *by* language, not the point of origin of symbolic production.

The fundamental discoveries of modern linguistics and psychoanalysis—discoveries made possible by the opening of the gap between signifier and signified—had a radical effect on the understanding of the operations of signifying systems. The light thrown on the enigma constituted by meaning as well as by society and identity came from the relationship discovered between them. That there is no reserve or "origin" of meaning, only the continuous production of signification, that "no meaning is sustained by anything other than reference to other meaning" (Jacques Lacan), made possible a study of the relations of the signifiers themselves in the production of meaning. The same is true for iconic sign systems as illustrated in Umberto Eco's analysis of his drawing of a horse:

> If I take a pen and draw on a sheet of paper the silhouette of a horse, through creating this silhouette by the extension of a single, elementary line of ink, everyone will be prepared to recognize a horse in my drawing; and yet the one property which the horse in the drawing has (a continuous black line) is the sole property which the real horse does not have. My drawing consists of a sign, which delineated "the space within = horse" and separates it from the "space without = non-horse," whereas the horse does not possess this property—therefore I have produced on my drawing not one condition of perception; for I perceive the horse on the basis of a large number of stimuli, not one of which is distantly comparable to the extended line. . . . Iconic signs reproduce a few conditions of perception, but only when these have been selected on the basis of codes of recognition and explained on the basis of graphic conventions.

The symbolic order is thus both the source of all meaning and, as Fredric Jameson points out, "the source of all cliche, the very fountainhead of all those more debased 'meaning-effects' which saturate our culture." To accept the text, to remain within the symbolic function ("By symbolic function we mean a system of signs organized into logico-syntactic structures whose goal is to accredit social communication as exchange purified of pleasure—a training process, an inhibition, which begins with the first echolalias, but fully imposes itself with the learning of language"—Julia Kristeva), is to be subject of others' discourse—hence tributary of a universal law. The privileged metaphor for this universal law Lacan has designated as the "Law of the Father," a term used to convey the notion of language as the cultural origin of law, as embodied by the myth of the father as figure of the law. Lacan links the individual's entry into language with Freud's theory of the acquisition of culture which takes place at the resolution of the Oedipal crisis with the capitulation to the father. To enter or acquire culture is to embrace simultaneously the symbolic order of language and the "Law of the Father" at the cost of repressing what is termed variously the discourse of the Other, the desire in language, or what for the French feminist theorists of female 'difference' is the female.

At the same time, to accept the text is to be granted a set of securities, to partake in that collective consumption regulated by the contingencies of society. To reject the text is to find oneself alien, silent or exposed to the psychosis that appears on the signifying borders of our culture. The only alternative is to seek the *pleasure* of the text, either by playing upon the codes already in place, or by finding passages through them, in a word the French recently have reactivated in English—jouissance.

It is the potential of this jouissance, this play of the signifiers themselves that the exhibition "The Revolutionary Power of Women's Laughter" intends to explore. It is not then a study in the comic, nor of laughter as invective, but an investigation into the function of language and the discourse that attempts to account for it—the logic of those systems and relations that create an identity for a sentence, a sign, an individual. The analysis of how meaning is produced and organized undermines the structures of domination in this form of society (call it the paternal, the phallic, the symbolic), and shatters its belief in a transparent text, an 'innocent' uncoded experience of a 'real' world, in the notion that language or any other form of symbolic production simply expresses 'things as they are.' The aim is both to dismantle the presumption of the 'innocence' of the signifying system and to explore the only signifying strategy which allows the speaking subject to shift the limits of its enclosure—through play, jouissance, laughter. "A code cannot be destroyed, only played off" (Barthes).

The exhibition constitutes a reading of the text which is no longer consumption, but play. The works do not postulate a new set of meanings or values, rather they function as visual or verbal puns, irruptions in the production of meaning and what is the same thing, the idea of value. The exhibition also points to the more radical potential of this play, suggested, although not developed in Saussure's theories, since the signifier can have an active function in creating and determining the signified.

Such an attitude towards language constitutes a wreckage of the symbolic order. And, while as Kristeva suggests, it may be necessary to be a woman "to take up that 'exorbitant wager' of carrying the project to the outer borders of the signifying venture of men," it should be clear that the feminist 'we' addressed by this exhibition is not gender exclusive. For we (both male and female) are governed by a monotheism whose essence is best expressed in metaphors of *The Book of Genesis*—the Word in the beginning, creating and dividing. And any revolutionary activity which addresses the logic of production (class) and reproduction (family) and which attempts neither an analysis of the construction of sexual difference, nor posits an alternative economy of the sexes is naive to the point of complicity. Thus the 'we' that this exhibition addresses is that audience who realizes that it is not only women who have been negatively inscribed within the hidden agenda of language. "The tremendous cultural revolution implied by this interior revolution of technique tickles the very heart and liver of a man, makes him feel good. Good, that is, if he isn't too damn tied to his favorite stupidities. That is why he laughs. His laugh is the first acknowledgement of liberation" (William Carlos Williams' response to Gertrude Stein's wholesale dismantling of the symbolic order).

This exhibition includes the work of six artists: Mike Glier, Ilona Granet, Jenny Holzer, Mary Kelly, Barbara Kruger, and Nancy Spero. Generally speaking, Kelly and Spero explore the realm of language prior to the construction of meaning, or, more accurately, where meaning occurs but has not yet become closure—the language of the child, the gesture, the maternal body—the realm of nonsense and desire; whereas Glier, Granet, Holzer, and Kruger play upon the codes already in place—the reality which has already been written.

Mary Kelly's *Post-Partum Document* forms the basis of the exhibition historically as well as theoretically. The work, begun in 1973 with the birth of her child, is an extended documentation of the child's entry into the symbolic order, experienced by the mother as loss—both of the child and her own initial 'loss' or negative entry into language and culture. "The whole project, not only of the visible art work but the process itself is about the relation of writing to the mother's body" (Kelly).

A complex nexus of psychoanalytic discourse (the only discourse on sexuality that exists) and historical materialism (the sexual division of labor and power), the *Post-Partum Document* is of seminal importance in the development of this culture's construction of the feminine. Although Kelly uses male maps (particularly the psychoanalytic theories of Lacan) to limn woman's position within a male terrain (the symbolic), this is not an act of complicity, for she undertakes what both Freud and Lacan either neglected or avoided: The entire *Post-Partum Document* is the articulation of the process of the creation of femininity. And, as Kelly points out, "in so far as the feminine is *said*, it is profoundly subversive." Thus, while theorized, as female sexuality always is, within masculine parameters, the theory is displaced in the work by its materialist distance from this ideology of the 'natural.' 'Femininity' is revealed not as a natural or essential but as a complicated edifice which the patriarchy constructs in order to represent 'masculinity' as power. The work is extremely restrained, there is no attack, no invective, its entire subversive impact comes from its revelation that what is natural, therefore inevitable, or evitable, therefore natural, is in fact arbitrary and therefore possible to change.

Jenny Holzer's *Truisms* and *Inflammatory Essays* disrupt the mechanisms by which language, encountered in the environment, creates the identity of the reader. They function much like the parable of the grotesque that Sherwood Anderson gives at the beginning of his novel, *Winesburg, Ohio*.

That in the beginning when the world was young there were a great many thoughts but no such thing as a truth. Man made the truths himself and each truth was a composite of a great many vague thoughts.

And then the people came along. Each as he appeared snatched up one of the truths. It was the truths that made the people grotesques. The old man had quite an elaborate theory concerning the matter. It was his notion that the moment one of the people took one of the truths to himself, called it his truth, and tried to live his life by it, he became a grotesque and the truth he embraced became a falsehood.

The *Inflammatory Essays* and *Truisms* arrest the consumer of language in the act of conformity, in the conditioned acceptance of some truisms, some authoritative statement, some adage by which one habitually conducts one's life. The *Truisms* function like Flaubert's *Dictionary of Accepted Ideas*: "Don't place too much trust in experts," "Don't run people's lives for them," "Children are the hope of the future." It is in the sheer multiplicity of these truths and the rapidity with which the viewer is presented with the next, equally valid, but often contradictory truth ("Children are the cruelest of all") that the radical displacement of Holzer's work inheres. The *Inflammatory Essays* are couched in the language of the *Book of Ecclesiastes* and set in the typeface of the *New York Times* headlines but the authority of the text is undermined by the conflicting truths of the message which moves the reader in and out of the realm of the absurd. It is the site of the construction of meaning and, by extension, the construction of the speaking subject that Holzer's work dismantles. Holzer is, as one critic put it, "the taxonomer of ideology, collecting 'what is' for immolation."

Ilona Granet does with the iconic sign system what Holzer does with the verbal. Granet makes her living as a sign painter where her job is to arrest the attention of people who "don't want to stop, don't want to read . . . it's all about no-time and that's it" (Granet). She works every day with the codes of signage. In fact, she, like other sign painters, works from a text called *The Sign Painter's Dictionary of Signs* in which the symbols that surround us are standardized. Her four monolithic male authority figures are, she says, "all about what I'm supposed to be advertising," and they are executed in exactly the same codes. The corporate landowner, and the gas-masked figure are taken from *Gentleman's Quarterly* and the general comes from *Forbes Magazine*—these figures are a collection of codes by which this culture denotes male success, male power. The figures are framed at top and bottom by two huge missiles—"These guys are really comfortable in that space, aren't they? I mean, other figures, if you put them between two missiles wouldn't look so relaxed" (Granet).

Nancy Spero's work is closely aligned to Mary Kelly's in that it suggests an alternative inscription of the female. The three works in the exhibition: "To The Revolution," "The First Language" and "Let The Priests Tremble" are hand-painted scrolls of images and sometimes collaged texts which are evocations of a new language of gesture and rhythm. "Let The Priests Tremble" interweaves a quote from Helene Cixous' "The Laugh of the Medusa" ("Let the priests tremble, we are going to show them our sexts! Too bad for them if they fall apart discovering that women aren't men, or that the mother doesn't have one.") with images of women's bodies. One work is a celebration of *difference*: "The grace and hope for freedom in the women's bodies is what I'm about" (Spero). "The First Language" is significantly without language, it is the attempt to embody the desire in language, the jouissance of the female body: ". . . there is play. There are dance-like figures, some triumphant figures—gestures of freedom—of the freedom of play" (Spero).

Barbara Kruger's work addresses the pictorial sign as site of the cultural construction of gender—more specifically: woman as image, man as bearer of the look. This is accomplished through a syntactical shift in the enunciative apparatus of photography. Kruger does not assume the role of creative *producer* of the sign—the photographs are quotations of other photographs. Even in the selection of the line texts which accompany the found images, the "authority" of the "source" is cited—the statements are compilations of the idees recues of advertising, military sloganeering, normative aesthetic theory and sexual stereotyping. The juxtaposed texts and images, removed from their "origin," from their seemingly "natural" position within the received systems of meaning, enter the realm of commentary; the gesture is that of "bearing the device."

Mike Glier's four paintings of shouting women are another syntactical shift—this time in the tradition of male artist and passive female model. These women are not silent objects of the gaze. In the context of the exhibition; Glier is given the last laugh—but the joke is on no one.

When the most solid guarantee of our identity—syntax—is revealed as a limit, the entire history of the western subject and his relationship to his enunciation has come to an end.
Julia Kristeva

Jo-Anna Isaak received her doctorate from the University of Toronto, Canada. She teaches in the Department of English, University of California, Santa Barbara, California. Currently, she is working on a book entitled "The Revolutionary Power of Women's Laughter."

Essay for *The Revolutionary Power of Women's Laughter* 1982